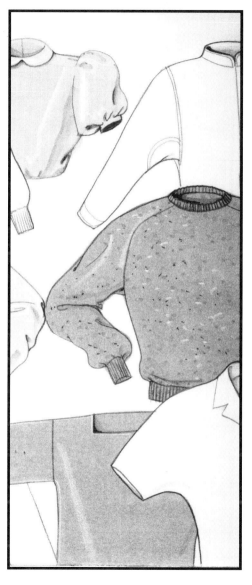

CONTENTS

ACKNOWLEDGMENTS

A book of this scope depends on a special pool of talents. From conceptual stage to finished book, *Design without Limits* involved many individuals working together, contributing their creative best.

Olga Kontzias, executive editor; Beth Applebome, assistant production editor; Adam Bohannon, art director; and Priscilla Taguer, production manager at Fairchild Publications who saw this publication as an opportunity to serve the fashion needs of consumers with special clothing needs.

Elizabeth Mauro, alumna of the fashion program at Drexel, who implemented and coordinated the earliest efforts for publication of this book.

Experts in the field of clothing for the handicapped: Joanne Boles, PhD, Kay Caddel, Adeline M. Hoffman, PhD, Audrey Newton, PhD, Naomi Reich, PhD, and Muriel Zimmerman.

The National Endowment for the Arts, especially Debbie Hoover, Bert Kubli, and Paula Terry.

Clothing designers and manufacturers: Bonnie Cashin, Stephen

Maniello, Albert and Pearl Nipon, Carole Stein-Hochman, Yeohlee Teng, and Stanley Tuttleman.

Private donors and foundations: International Ladies Garment Workers' Union (now Union of Needletrades, Industrial and Textile Employees (UNITE)), Mrs. J. Maxwell Moran, Mrs. Anne Reimel, Samuel S. Fels Foundation, The Sun Company, and William Penn Foundation.

Other special persons: Ken Brier, Sylvia Clark, Mary Epstein, Jonathan Estrin, Phyllis Feldkamp, Cynthia Friedman, Bonnie Gellman, Lucinda Hathaway, Brian Hawkins, Judith Mangel, Mary Jane Matranga, Cynthia Minuti, Jacques Naugle, Louise Ott, Bernard Sagik, Florence Weinstein, and Bart Weitz, PhD.

Winifred Curtis, Dolores' first design assistant.

And: Rita, Lisa, and Kevin Parry, Dolores' family; Charlotte Weiss and Fred, Danielle, and Jesse, Renée's collective heart.

PREFACE

Renée Weiss Chase

The Americans with Disabilities Act, passed by Congress in 1990, helped more disabled individuals enter the mainstream. Accessibility is the law and those with physical limitations now can participate in nearly every facet of business, entertainment, education and culture—opportunities that might have been unavailable just over a decade ago. With increased accessibility comes the ever-present human need to look great. Appearance has a powerful impact on an individual's personal well being and their acceptance by others.

One of the purposes of this book is to show the public that clothing for the physically disabled can be as stylish, sophisticated, and current as the work done by any "Seventh Avenue" designer. Another purpose is to provide information that will allow the designer, seamstress, or tailor to address the disabled person's special clothing problems in an easy and organized way.

Drexel University professor M. Dolores Quinn discovered that fashionable as well as functional clothing is strongly desired by the disabled community, but it is generally unavailable. In 1977, the Design Department at Drexel University established a Fashion Design Research

Studio to study the clothing needs of the physically disabled. Under the direction of Professor Quinn, a course was developed and offered to senior and graduate fashion design students.

At first, disabled individuals voluntarily assisted in this project, which was called "Designs within Limits." Involvement spread to several local rehabilitation hospitals, and many individuals contacted the research studio for assistance. A network of people interested in these special clothing problems began to emerge. Physical and occupational therapists wanted to make the clothing available to their patients and clients. Designers and entrepreneurs became interested in a potentially profitable market. Relatives of disabled persons sought ways to answer the clothing needs of their loved ones. Home economists continued to conduct similar research at various colleges and universities.

A number of small grants and donations assisted Drexel in keeping the project alive. In 1978, the first of three grants from the National Endowment for the Arts (NEA) was awarded to further research in this area. A variety of prototype garments were designed for a wide array of physical disabilities. The Fashion Design Research Studio received national attention when an article about Designs within Limits appeared in *The New York Times*. The syndication of this article resulted in increased interest in the project. The need for this specialized clothing was confirmed repeatedly.

As staff and students continued to develop new prototypes, it was realized that the design possibilities for fashionable, functional clothing for the disabled were not limited as much by the client's physical handicap as by the designer's imagination. The name of the project was proudly changed from "Designs within Limits" to "Design *without* Limits."

In 1982, the National Fashion Competition for the Physically Disabled was conducted under the sponsorship of NEA and Drexel University. Designers and students throughout the United States and Canada were invited to submit clothing designs, which answered the needs of the disabled. The results ranged from a covering for a premature baby, to a garment for a stroke victim, to a necklace for a person with arthritis. The entries reflected how diverse and enormous in scope these special clothing problems are. Two important conclusions were derived from the competition. First, the physically disabled are extremely diverse in the range of their disabilities. Second, they are also diverse in the physical limitations resulting from those disabilities. To tackle the clothing concerns for the entire group was too vast a study for one project. The study and this book were then focused on persons using wheelchairs, crutches and prostheses, and on persons with limited mobility.

In 1990 Simplicity Pattern Company joined Drexel University in publishing the first edition of this book, *Simplicity's Design without Limits*. Well over 10,000 copies were printed and each one was sold.

Libraries, hospital groups, and friends and family members of persons with disabilities called about purchasing this book. However, there were none to be had except via interlibrary loan. Over the next five years, hundreds of inquiries were made regarding book purchases. Numerous publishers were contacted regarding reprinting the book; none took the risk until Olga Kontzias, the executive editor at Fairchild Books, took the project under her wing.

This revised first edition published by Fairchild includes some changes and updates. The resource list is updated and the reading list includes additional books and booklets, but most of the book remains the same. Professor Quinn's philosophy is as valid today as it was twenty-five years ago. Clothing for the disabled need not be clinical or unattractive—beautiful clothing can adorn the disabled as well as the able-bodied. This book documents the ideas and solutions developed in Drexel's Fashion Design Research Studio. It is certainly not the answer to all the clothing problems of the disabled. But it is a springboard for coping with those problems and for educating the general public about paying attention to a group of individuals whose fashion needs have long been overlooked—not just by the design community but even by the individuals themselves.

M. Dolores Quinn

The ideas presented in this book first took shape more than twenty-five years ago when I presented a paper at an Association of College Professors of Textiles and Clothing (ACPTC) conference in Dallas, Texas. (In 1991 the name of this organization was changed to the International Textile and Apparel Association (ITAA).) The essence of that paper follows:

"I believe that clothing is an art form and therefore must always be constructed from the finest and most appropriate materials. It must be imaginative and exquisitely crafted so that it can be worn comfortably on the body and removed with ease. Clothing must enhance and fit the human form both when the body is static and when it is in motion. As it supports the body, clothing must in itself be visually handsome and must be subordinate to the person wearing it. Clothing also must enhance the character and beauty of the wearer."

Whether we are businesspeople, athletes, children, socialites, or clergy, we all have an image of ourselves that we maintain and present to the world around us. We expect to present an image of competence, mental and spiritual health, and social appropriateness. Everybody has some physical imperfection or limitation. The longer I worked on this project, the more difficult it was to distinguish those with physical limitations from those without limitations. Whether we are at the peak of our physical abilities or not, we want to look and feel our best and present ourselves well. Clothes must be well-constructed, manageable, durable, and fashionable. Why not make the most of our attributes? Why not design without limits and dress within our limits?

Since the Fashion Design Research Studio was established, this project has been a springboard for new insights into clothing design for the disabled community. It provided me with many intellectual and creative design ideas and stimulated my thinking in many other areas. Clothing designers have contributed their suggestions and have been stimulated to produce new designs based on disabled clients' needs. Clothing manufacturers have discovered new markets with customers who have purchasing power. Now that disabled individuals have fewer legal barriers and more access to employment opportunities, transportation, and cultural excursions, they need attractive and comfortable clothes to wear while pursuing these opportunities.

I have met many talented and profoundly generous people through this project. I first met Renée Weiss Chase when she was a freshman in my class at Drexel University, and we worked together in the Fashion Design Research Studio and on this book. She has made significant contributions to this project and has been a shining star. Throughout the years, we have enjoyed a close friendship and an enriching professional experience. Without Renée's contributions, this project would not be where it is today. There are many others whom I have not yet met, but I hope they will benefit from the ideas and the challenges presented in this book.

RESOURCES

Hard To Find Notions and Supplies

The Button Shop
P.O. Box 1065
Oak Park, IL 60304
(708) 795-1234
Hard to find sewing supplies, zippers cut to order. Catalog $1.00 refundable.

Clotilde, Inc.
1909 SW First Avenue
Ft. Lauderdale, FL 33315-2100
(800) 772-2891
www.clotilde.com
Sewing notions and supplies.

The Fabric Club
1050 Northfield Court
Suite 365
Roswell, GA 30076
www.fabricclub.com
Sewing supplies and notions.

Nancy's Notions
333 Beichl Avenue
P.O. Box 683
Beaver Dam, WI 53916-0683
(800) 833-0690
www.nancysnotions.com
Sewing notions and supplies.

Newark Dressmaker Supply
6473 Ruch Road
P.O. Box 20730
Lehigh Valley, PA 18002-0730
(800) 736-6783
Sewing notions and supplies. Zippers cut to order.

Professional Sewing Supplies
P.O. Box 14272
Seattle, WA 98114-4272
(206) 324-8823
www.sewexpo.com
Sewing supplies and notions. For catalog send 25¢ self-addressed stamped envelope.

Cooperative Extensions/Foundations

Alabama Cooperative Extension System
Auburn University
104 Duncan Hall
Auburn University
Auburn, AL 36849
(334) 844-4444
Brochure of helpful resources.

Arthritis Foundation
New York Chapter
122 East 42nd Street
New York, NY 10168
(212) 984-8700
www.arthritis.org
Brochure includes a resource listing of self-help publications and medical information series booklets.

Disabled Living Foundation
380-384 Harrow Road
London W9 2HU, England
(020) 7289-6111
www.dlf.org.uk
Provides publications, advice, and assistance for those with disabilities.

Easter Seals
National Headquarters
230 West Monroe Street
Suite 1800
Chicago, IL 60606-4802
www.easter-seals.org
Offers resources and opportunities to people with disabilities.

Iowa State Cooperative Extension
Iowa State University
Ames, IA 50011
(515) 294-5247
www.extension.iastate.edu
Brochure of helpful resources.

P.R.I.D.E.
391 Long Hill Road
Groton, CT 06340
(860) 445-1448
Catalog of helpful tips for adjusting ready-to-wear, resource for patterns, etc.

Special Aids and Clothing for the Disabled

Adrian's Closet
P.O. Box 65
San Marcos, CA 92079
(800) 831-2577
www.adrianscloset.com
Aids for easier living.

Fashion Ease
Division of M & M Health Care Apparel Co.
1541 60th Street
Brooklyn, NY 11219
(800) 221-8929
Easy to fit clothing.

Sammons Preston, Inc.
AbilityOne Corporation
4 Sammons Court
Bolingbrook, IL 60440
(800) 323-5547
www.sammonspreston.com
Household aids, dressing aids, and foot care products.

Clothing Catalogues

American Health Care Apparel Ltd.
302 Town Center Boulevard
Easton, PA 18040
(800) 252-0584

Anitavee's Adaptive Apparel
3000B East Main Street
Suite 277
Columbus, OH 43209
(888) 246-8203
www.anitavee.com

Buck and Buck, Inc.
3111 27th Avenue South
Seattle, WA 98144-6502
(800) 458-0600
www.buckandbuck.com

Personal Touch Health Care Apparel
P.O. Box 230321
Brooklyn, NY 11223
(718) 375-1703
www.nursinghomeapparel.com

Professional Fit Clothing
831 North Lake Street
Suite 1
Burbank, CA 91502
(800) 422-2FIT
www.professionalfit.com

Special Clothes: Beautiful Clothing for Children with Special Needs
P.O. Box 333
Harwich, MA 02645
(508) 896-7939
www.special-clothes.com

Wardrobe Wagon
555 Valley Road
West Orange, NJ 07052
(800) 992-2737
www.wardrobewagon.com

Chapter 1

How This Book Evolved

When we started this research project, when we started thinking about a book in general and *Design Without Limits* in particular, terminology was a great issue. Were the clients to be called physically handicapped or physically disabled—what was the appropriate word?

Before the project could be undertaken, the proper terms had to be chosen. An occupational therapist who was interviewed during the project suggested that a disability is of a physical nature and a handicap is a state of mind.

Disability is of a physical nature; a handicap is a state of mind.

1

Disabled persons need not consider themselves handicapped.

An able-bodied person can be handicapped while a disabled person may not be handicapped at all. A handicap is a measure of our own self-perception.

Psychologically, this definition opens the possibility for personal potential in all human beings, whether able-bodied or disabled. The term "handicapped" will therefore not be used here.

The primary goal of this book is to provide guidelines for the design and production of fashionable and functional clothing for the disabled. But who *are* the disabled? In order to begin the clothing study, a working definition of the term "disabled" had to be stated.

> **A disabled person is anyone who does not have full functional mobility.**

This means that the person is unable to perform the typical daily tasks that are required in leading a "normal life." "Normal life" is a relative term and varies with the individual, but for these purposes it simply means the physical func-

Holistic—the principle that a part is understandable only in relation to the whole.

Occupational therapist—one who uses selected creative activities to help patients recover from injury or illness.

Aesthetic sensibilities—Having a sense or love of beauty.

Incontinent—unable to control bowel or bladder functions.

Adaptive clothing—Ready-to-wear clothing which is specifically constructed for use by the disabled.

Notions—small articles for use in sewing, such as buttons, zippers, etc.

tions required to move freely and care for one's own well-being.

Under this definition it is clear that the disabled are an enormous group of diverse people with a wide range of needs and weaknesses. This book cannot answer all of those needs, but the ideas presented here can be applied to many more specific problems than are illustrated in the text.

THE RESULTS OF DISABILITY

Reduced or impaired mobility can be the result of disease, spinal cord injury, stroke, amputation, accident or impact, but two people with spinal cord injuries will rarely have identical disabilities. Persons with arthritis will probably have completely different physical capabilities. Similar causes do not necessarily result in similar disabilities. However, similar disabilities can be the result of different causes. For example, limited finger movement can be the result of arthritis or an accident involving nerve damage to the hand.

We cannot look at the clothing needs of the disabled by looking at the *cause* of their disability. The common factor for a clothing study is not a particular disease, but the physical changes that are the result of that disease. Obviously, clothing for all spine-injured people cannot be the same; by the same token, clothing for all arthritics cannot be the same. Garments must be designed to answer the problems caused by the disease or injury.

When we examine the impact of various disabilities, it seems most individuals fall into one of two classes of physical posture: the **seated figure** and the **standing figure**. This is a very simplified way to study disabilities as they relate to changes in body form and posture; it is the first piece of information to be considered before examining specific problems that accompany a particular disability.

Each disabled person must be seen as an individual with a distinct set of physical and psychological limitations; and each garment designed and produced for that individual must take all of those limitations into account. This is a well-rounded approach involving the person's physical and mental abilities. Even though this book is primarily divided into two main parts (the seated figure and the standing figure), we must emphasize that all of the aspects of a particular limitation must be taken into account when planning a garment design. This is the way to approach design in general, whether creating clothing, furniture, or interior space. First, the consumer is identified and his or her particular needs are isolated; then the design is completed based on this set of limitations.

THE PSYCHOLOGICAL IMPACT OF CLOTHING

Each person must be seen holistically, in relation to all of his or her needs, before a garment design can be planned. It is important to consider not only the physical needs and limitations of that individual, but also the psychological impact that a disability can have upon that person.

All human beings develop their first sense of self from their own bodies. They understand "who they are" based upon what they can do on a physical level. As we grow up, our physical sense of self expands to include the intellectual and the social. Our self-perception is strongly affected by how others view us. The two combined perceptions, physical and social, result in an individual's self esteem.

When a person becomes disabled the perception of self is often confused, damaged, or even lost. Becoming disabled can be experienced as if a death had occurred—the person goes through grief and mourning. This process hopefully results in some sort of resolution and acceptance of the disability and a willingness to rebuild a sense of self and self-esteem. It is then that the wish to look "normal" surfaces. During an interview with an occupational therapist at Moss Rehabilitation Center in Philadelphia, the grieving process was discussed. The therapist said that once patients start exhibiting a concern about clothing and appearance, she knows that they are well on the road to psychological recovery. This concern for looking "normal" and being socially

A person who becomes disabled may go through a period of grief and mourning before adjusting.

Comfortable and fashionable clothing can provide self-esteem.

acceptable is a milestone in the recovery process.

The psychological impact of clothing has been the topic of many books and research projects. The positive effect of clothing on self-esteem, productivity and performance has been strongly and clearly established. For example, studies have shown that disabled children are more clothes-conscious than able-bodied children. Other research has indicated that in a rehabilitation setting there is a significant rise in the self-esteem of patients, after fashionable, functional clothing is developed for them.

On a physical level, living with disability is a very complex process; on a psychological level it is an even greater struggle. If a large part of "normalcy" hinges upon positive self-esteem, and clothing can help to provide that self-esteem, then great energy and support should be provided to make appropriate clothing available. According to the therapist at Moss Rehabilitation Center, many patients feel that ill-fitting, con-stricting clothing is just part of the suffering that they must endure as disabled people. *Of course, this is simply not the case!*

DESIGN CONSIDERATIONS

Every design problem has its own limitations. These limitations define the problem and provide the basis for the designer's solution. The success of the product is a measure of how well the designer blends aesthetics and technical expertise to solve the design problem.

Designing clothing for the disabled requires the combination of many skills and experiences:

- Aesthetic sensibilities (this will be discussed at length in Chapter Two).

- Fashion awareness.

- Basic technical skills—a working knowledge of fabrics, patternmaking and construction (see Chapter Six).

- Individual needs and preferences of the wearer.

- Input from therapists who have worked with similar problems.

- Input from medical personnel who deal with the problem on a clinical level.

- Input from the disabled, who experience shared difficulties.

There are many books available on the subject of design and visual thinking. Information on patternmaking and construction also abounds. (See the reading list on pages 94–95 for useful books and booklets on these subjects.) Many researchers have written about clinical and functional needs of the disabled and the medical problems that arise when these needs are not answered. The combination of all of this information is what has been lacking. Fashion or good design need not be sacrificed for a functional garment. There is no reason why a dress for an incontinent woman who needs easy access to a collection bag cannot be as fashionable as any well-designed dress found on the racks of a major department store. Her clothing should be functional —comfortable, easy to put on and take off, and easy to maintain. It should also be beautiful—quality material that is lovely to touch and in a color and style that compliments her body and complexion.

Adaptive or institutional clothing is clinical in nature and appearance. It calls attention to itself and the wearer in a negative way because it addresses the disability rather than the person wearing the garment. In other words, adaptive clothing is not designed with fashion as a priority; it is designed only with the disability in mind. The integration of all of the elements necessary for a complete design has not been achieved in most adaptive clothing; the disabled customer has little choice but to buy what is available, or sacrifice function for the discomfort of fashion.

When an able-bodied person goes into a clothing store, he or she can make many choices. The disabled rarely have these choices. We hope this book will help to broaden the opportunities and availabilities open to all.

THE PAST AND THE FUTURE

Clothing for the disabled community is not a new issue. Research began on the subject in the 1950s following World War II and the Korean War. But until the 1970s attention was concentrated on adaptive clothing rather than fashionable clothing. In the last 10 years fashion has grown in importance in this area. Researchers, clinicians, and home economists have become better equipped to deal with design and production issues.

Although sharing of information and product availability has been limited, now there is a commitment to a clearinghouse for information on clothing for the dis-abled (Reich). Many bright, dedicated scholars have published the results of their clothing research in rehabilitative and medical journals. A growing number of mail order companies are currently offering garments which are both adaptive and fashionable, as well as appropriate notions and accessories (see Resources, pages xi–xiii).

Ways of providing this information to the disabled are still being developed; rehabilitation centers are beginning to become involved. But it is still up to the disabled and their families to seek out this information and to educate themselves as much as possible about meeting their needs. Although appropriate ready-made garments may not always be available, the disabled person can still identify his or her needs (both function and aesthetic), find appropriate patterns and a dependable tailor or seamstress and begin the design process.

The Suggested Readings at the back of this book can help you find other sources of information.

Chapter 2

Design Principles

A substantial amount of literature has been written about altering clothing to suit the needs of the disabled. Guides are available to help disabled persons adapt their wardrobes into more functional form. (See the Resources list on pages xi–xiii.)

The solution to the clothing dilemma of the disabled, however, does not lie in coping with, adapting, or altering purchased clothing. The disabled community needs specially designed clothing. Whether the designer of this cloth-

The disabled community needs specially designed clothing.

7

Beauty is a necessary part of our lives, not something extra which may be added.

ing is an accomplished professional or a skilled home sewer, the goal is the same: the marriage of function and aesthetics—the production of workable yet beautiful garments.

André Courreges, a well-known French designer, made the statement: "Luxury in clothes to me has no meaning. It belongs to the past. My problem is not rich embroidery, useless lavishness—it is to harmoniously resolve function problems—just like the engineer who designs a plane—like the man who conceives a car."

Before the combination of function and aesthetics can take place, the basics of each must be understood. Only after this fundamental understanding is reached can the designer blend the two elements—function and aesthetics. This union, however, should be in the designer's mind from the very beginning of his or her design. When we consider the functionality of a garment, we focus on the physical requirements in dressing that are the result of a particular disability. Functionality is dis-cussed in later chapters in relation to the individual's particular disability and the requirements this disability places on clothing.

This chapter addresses the subject of aesthetics and establishes basic principles that you as the designer can use in creating clothes for the disabled. Many of the topics discussed in this chapter will be reviewed in later chapters.

We may begin by accepting as fact that beauty is one of our special needs, emotionally necessary for survival. Beauty is not something extra that might or might not be provided; it is a necessary ingredient in our lives. Creating a beautiful object, whether it ultimately hangs on a museum wall or is worn to work each day, is the goal of every designer.

VISUAL DESIGN

The same basic elements—line, space, form, texture, and color—are found in all visual design, whether the medium is cloth, leather, paint, or metal. Certain uses of an element give similar ef-fects under specific conditions. For example, a pale shade of blue/gray in a design can create a soothing, cooling effect. On the other hand, that same blue on a background of bright orange can completely change the mood. Selecting an appropriate color and combining it with other colors is a skill that requires artistic judgment, understanding of color phenomena, and an awareness of our own taste.

Developing an eye for color is a matter of knowledge and of practice. Begin to notice how you feel when you wear certain colors or see others in those colors. Try to see how the same clothing in a variety of colors can create a variety of effects. Experiment with different shades and patterns of fabrics until you feel comfortable making these choices.

The elements are not independent; they work together to produce the finished effect. Soon you will be able to understand each design element and its interaction with the others; you will develop awareness and creative strengths you didn't know you had.

Line

The line of a garment includes the direction that the outside edges take as well as all of the horizontals, diagonals and verticals within the body of the garment. The structural elements in a piece of clothing (yokes, panels, pockets, etc.) thus contribute to the overall line of that garment. Seams and darts determine the line of garments, as do decorative details—pockets, collars, and trimmings. The combinations of decisions regarding outside edges, placement of structural elements, and decorative details yield the "line" of a garment.

Line in clothing, however, must also be considered in relation to the line of the body that will wear it. Since a seated figure appears to be visually compressed, for example, the emphasis of a vertical line will provide an illusion of extra height. We will talk more about this in later sections of the book.

Shape

Shape is defined as a flat area enclosed by lines. Shapes within clothing can have desirable and undesirable aspects. Selecting and combining shapes in a successful garment is simplified when these visual effects are understood by the designer. The successful garment combines the shapes of the parts to form a pleasing whole whether the wearer is at rest or moving.

Basically, horizontal shapes add width, vertical shapes add height. The diagonal may take on the characteristics of either and will frequently camouflage figure irregularities. An untrained person may encounter difficulties in deciding which direction to choose. For example, horizontal stripes may *not* add width, especially if the contrast between colors is close, the stripes are fine, or if the total effect is one of "stacked" horizontals resulting in a vertical effect, much like a tall ladder with short horizontal steps.

The following guidelines may be used for any part of a garment; they should not be used where they will emphasize the wearer's negative features.

- A silhouette is emphasized by the direction of its dominant line: a slender, vertically-shaped style will heighten and narrow; a thick, horizontally-shaped style will shorten and widen. When subdividing a garment shape, especially for the placement of seams, pleats, armholes, necklines, and waistlines, the vertical lengthens; the horizontal widens. For example, when designing for a person in a wheelchair, use vertical design lines rather than horizontal, so that as much body-lengthening as possible is achieved. Horizontal yoke or pocket lines should be avoided. A better choice is long vertical seaming or decorative trim edging the garment vertically.

- Shapes extending far away from the body, whether hairstyles or garment parts such as full skirts or puffed sleeves, add apparent bulk and weight.

- Although loose-fitting clothes can sometimes add weight, they also can help camouflage figure

Horizontal stripes may add width.

Vertical stripes may add height.

See the color section at the end of this chapter for more color suggestions.

extremes of thinness and heaviness. A full-cut style may add apparent weight or size to a neighboring part of the body as well as to the part it covers.

- Closely-fitted garments emphasize actual body contours and usually increase apparent size.

- Curved shapes counter angularity; straightness counters rotundity. In other words, soft, rounded lines help a very thin angular person look fuller, and straight, geometric design lines help a plump person look less round.

- A shape tends to emphasize that part of the body at which it ends. If the hemline of a jacket ends at the widest part of the pelvis, the hips are the part of the body that will be emphasized. Therefore, it is important to be concerned with where the edge of a garment lies on a particular body, especially since most clothing edges are horizontal.

Color

In selecting colors, the designer must decide whether smooth harmony, strong variation or multicolor intensity is desired. Color must be chosen carefully for it has greater influence on our emotions than any other design element except pattern. The dominant color in a garment or ensemble draws the most attention and sets the mood for the wearer's overall appearance. The dominant color is the one that attracts the strongest and most immediate attention. Accent colors draw attention to specific areas and complement or enhance the dominant color. Subordinate colors tend to blend in with either the accent or dominant color rather than make a statement of their own. All colors—dominant, subordinate and accent —must, of course, blend into an appealing whole and complement the wearer's skin and hair tones.

The principle of drawing attention to the positive features and away from negative ones, whether the wearer is physically limited or not, can easily be addressed through color. Dark, dull colors tend to thin the body and not attract attention. Therefore, someone with heavy proportions in the lower half of the body may want to consider wearing dark skirts or trousers. In the case of the wheelchair-bound person, for example, attention should be drawn away from the afflicted body part through the use of a dark color scheme in that area.

Light colors can be young and soft, but they can also expand the shape. Bright, warm colors are aggressive and should be worn where attention is desirable. Neutral colors, whether light or dark, tend to minimize attention to a specific area.

The psychological impact of color should not be underestimated. Happy colors, like red, sunflower yellow, or orange, lift the spirits not only of the wearer, but of the observer. Small touches of bright accent color liven up an outfit, so the use of a bright necktie or lively beads can lift a garment tremendously.

For a clearer understanding of the principles underlying the use of color, some vocabulary will be helpful:

- The *value* of a particular color is its degree of lightness or darkness. Try holding 3 or 4 pieces of black fabric next to each other to appreciate the varying values.

- *Hue* is simply another word for color or shade, but it implies recognition between subtle differences of shades. Blue, for instance, is not a very descriptive term if the hue is not mentioned. Is it navy, royal, cobalt, etc.? Cool hues (gray-blue, for example) tend to recede, while warmer hues come forward.

- *Intensity* refers to the brightness of a hue. Pink, for example, may range in brightness from pale, baby pink, to strong, hot pink. Vivid intensity demands attention, while neutral intensity is less assertive.

With this knowledge one can begin to experiment and to use color in ways that go beyond the guides in this *Color* segment. Initially, it was stated that dark colors minimize and light colors maximize. Consequently, a heavy person might select navy blue rather than powder blue. This is a decision based on the value of the color. When hue and intensity are also taken into consideration, this plumpish person could also select a light shade of blue with a cool hue and neutral intensity. Therefore, a grayish blue would be appropriate as would a pale teal blue or ice blue. Turquoise or royal blue might be less appropriate because the intensity of these hues is strong and demands attention.

This is not to say that a heavy person should never wear a bright color. The rules mentioned here are not hard and fast and established rules are often broken. The designer must take into account the *amount* and *placement* of each color used in a garment as well as the personal taste of the wearer. Experimenting with unusual combinations of colors can often yield very positive results, so use it fearlessly as part of your design.

Texture

Texture plays a special role as a design element because it is the very element that applies to the senses of touch, sight, and even sound. The human body has its own textures that invite comparison and contrast. Skin may be smooth, fine, porous, or wrinkled. Satin would flatter a fine, smooth skin but would make a porous or wrinkled one look even more irregular. A fabric with a nubby texture would repeat and emphasize very curly hair, but may be more interesting with wavy or straight hair. Crinkled textures might emphasize blemished skin. Opaque fabrics with a smooth surface and firm textures show less comparison to skin texture. Clothing textures very similar to, or very different from, personal body textures will emphasize those personal textures. Choose or avoid these fabric texture extremes accordingly.

Clothing textures interact with each other and with body shape, creating illusions (bulk, filminess,

Experiment with unusual color combinations to find the best choices.

Fabric textures can enhance skin and hair.

etc.) or accenting reality. For the disabled, the surface qualities of fabric become important because physical comfort is, in many ways, dependent on the *hand* or feel of the fabric used in the garment. The person who has little sensation in his or her legs places great trust in the texture of the fabric chosen for pants or skirt. Friction between the garment and the body must be avoided to prevent the disastrous problem of pressure sores.

In other instances, surface quality of fabric can work for a disabled person by using the dimensional aspect of the fabric to camouflage figure irregularities. For example, a woman with scoliosis may select a fabric with a deep pile such as fleece or bouclé to "even out" her body's asymmetry. Psychologically, the effects of wearing a plush or luxurious cloth can heighten the mood and self-concept, not only of the wearer, but of his or her audience.

Fabric Patterns

Pattern is an arrangement of line, space, and shape that contains color. More simply, pattern is a design woven or knitted in or printed on a fabric. Patterned fabric commands attention more quickly than plain fabric. Even bold structural lines can be lost in the presence of strong pattern. Concern then must be given to the size and placement of the pattern on the garment. Ten observations gathered by Marian Davis in her book, *Visual Design in Dress,* are helpful considerations when selecting patterned fabrics.

1. Fabric patterns accent the body part where they are used and tend to make the area seem larger.
2. The larger the motif size, the more enlarging the fabric pattern, although tiny patterns will not necessarily reduce.
3. Extremes of fabric pattern size emphasize extremes of figure size. Large motifs on a heavy person accent size by repetition, whereas a tiny pattern

emphasizes by contrast. A tiny motif on a petite person can be compatible; a large motif might overpower the wearer.

4. Directional fabric patterns emphasize that direction on the body and carry the effects of its straight or curved lines.

5. Extreme contrasts of color and line enlarge, whereas gentle contrasts do not.

6. Fabric patterns add visual interest to plain textures that might otherwise be boring.

7. Fabric patterns attract attention away from the silhouette and so can help distract from less than ideal body contours.

8. Fabric patterns can complement simple structural styling.

9. Sharply edged motifs are more forceful and enlarging than fuzzy-edged motifs, and make figure/background distinction easier.

10. Fabric patterns that create optical illusions soon become distracting.

If there are many seams and darts in the design of the garment, a small, uncomplicated fabric pattern should be used. Large, commanding fabric patterns require simple structural lines. The location and size of a motif depends on the size of the wearer. Obviously, a large motif placed on an area of the body that one wishes to minimize is self-defeating. But placing that motif on a well-proportioned part of the body emphasizes that part and minimizes the rest.

Using the positive effects of pattern is similar to using the other design elements. In essence, the task is to focus positive attention on the wearer. Use the elements of good design to draw the eye to the wearer's attractive features; attention will then be drawn away from the less desirable features. This is especially crucial for the disabled person. Bear in mind that the main purpose of clothing is to enhance the attractiveness of the wearers and make them feel good about themselves. Clothes should draw attention to the per-

Small geometric patterns are a good choice for the smaller figure.

Use color, texture and pattern to create the desired illusion.

son they cover, not to themselves. The wearer should dominate—not the clothes.

Once these design components are understood one can then begin to employ them to create an **illusion**—the illusion of a more "normal" appearance.

ILLUSION

For the disabled individual it is very important to be able to focus on the positive and distract from the negative, as well as to make the imperfect appear perfect. Good visual design can make this possible.

Texture, style, pattern, and color can all contribute to the illusion. It should be kept in mind, however, that using these elements to create illusions to enhance one body area can also create a problem in another area. A feeling for overall unity should constantly be a concern.

The following guide adapted from *Visual Design in Dress* can be of great help when trying to hide or accent physical features.

OVERALL HEIGHT

These styles can make the wearer look shorter:

☐ large hats and full or "permed" hair style

☐ short skirts, cuffed pants

☐ shoulder, midriff or hip yokes

☐ double breasted openings on jackets

☐ short, wide jackets

☐ boleros, vests

☐ full sleeves

☐ wide ties and lapels

☐ bloused bodices

☐ accents at waistline

☐ contrasting upper and lower garments

☐ wide or contrasting belts

☐ strong horizontal lines

☐ horizontal ruffles, flounces or shirring

These styles can make the wearer look taller, whether standing or seated in a wheelchair:

☐ short, close hairstyles

☐ small hat

☐ narrow, slim, or slightly flared pants or skirts

☐ sheath, shift, princess style dresses

☐ single-breasted jackets with shawl collars or narrow lapels

☐ longer jackets and full-length coats

☐ long bishop or shirt sleeves

☐ one-piece dresses

☐ diagonally-draped saris

☐ same color upper and lower garments

☐ narrow self-belts or no belt

☐ vertically unbroken structural design

☐ small-scale, all-over or vertical pattern

☐ neat, small details at the top, such as stand-up collars or shoulder yoke seaming

OVERALL WEIGHT

For the wheelchair-bound or otherwise disabled person, lack of exercise can lead to weight problems. The following styles can help provide an illusion of slimness:

☐ accent near face or neck

☐ narrow, long set-in or raglan sleeves

☐ chemise, princess, sheath, coachman styles

☐ single-breasted closings

☐ long pants, gently flared, long or gored skirts

☐ cooler hues

☐ medium dark values

☐ duller intensities

☐ thin or vertical lines

☐ straight lines, sharp angles

☐ narrow panels

☐ small-scale, vertical patterns

The following styles can add weight to figures which are too thin from illness or muscle atrophy:

☐ accent on heaviest part of body

☐ smocks or bloused bodices

☐ double-breasted jackets

☐ waist-length vests

☐ full, cropped pants

☐ gathered skirts or unpressed pleats

☐ warmer hues

☐ light, pastel values

☐ bright intensities

☐ thick accent at waistline

☐ horizontal lines

☐ midriff or hip yokes

☐ unbroken full curves, roundness

☐ wide panels

☐ large-scale, bold pattern

☐ fitted garments

Yoke—a shaped piece in a garment, fitted at the shoulders or hips, from which the garment hangs.

Ensemble—a person's entire costume.

Cool colors—colors relating to water or foliage, such as blues, greens and lavenders. These colors make us feel cooler.

Warm colors—colors relating to the sun, such as yellows, reds and oranges. These colors make us feel warmer.

Scoliosis—A curving condition of the spine.

Boucle—a fabric with a rough, nubby appearance.

Motif—a repeated element in a printed pattern; for example, a pattern with a leaf motif.

Bolero—A short open vest

Princess style—A dress or coat with vertical seaming over the bustline.

Dolman—a sleeve with a wide armhole and narrow cuff.

Use the tips in this section to select a flattering style.

Floral prints are soft and attractive; a large print re- quires simple lines in the garment.

SKELETAL CURVE

The following styles minimize spinal curvature:

- ☐ short simple hairstyles
- ☐ small earrings
- ☐ choker or no necklaces
- ☐ front neck interest
- ☐ high necks with front closings
- ☐ interesting shaped shoulder yokes or back bodice draping
- ☐ bloused bodice back
- ☐ dark values in shoulder area
- ☐ medium heavy, thick textures
- ☐ small-scale, all-over or vertical pattern

The following styles call attention to spinal curvature:

- ☐ full hairstyles or back chignon
- ☐ long necklaces, pendants, or scarves that make front look weighted down
- ☐ back neck accent
- ☐ low back necks or closings
- ☐ sailor or other collars flat in back
- ☐ straight lines or tucks at back shoulder
- ☐ tightly fitted bodices
- ☐ plain fabrics
- ☐ light values, bright colors in back shoulder area
- ☐ thin or shiny textures
- ☐ round lines in back shoulder area

BUST

The following styles minimize the bustline:

- [ ] straight-edge shoulder lines or collars
- [ ] high cowl necklines
- [ ] single-breasted openings
- [ ] vertical bodice stripes or tucks
- [ ] full skirts
- [ ] dark values, dull intensities
- [ ] medium textures
- [ ] bodices bloused at waist
- [ ] "Chanel" or loosely fitted jackets
- [ ] dominantly vertical collar style
- [ ] padded shoulders

These styles enhance a small bustline:

- [ ] jabot or long tie collar
- [ ] horizontal shoulder ruffles or pleats
- [ ] shoulder yoke with gathered bodice below
- [ ] bodice smocking, shirring, pleating, draping or gathering at bust
- [ ] bodices gently bloused at bust
- [ ] cuffs or sleeve fullness at bust
- [ ] dolman, cape, short bell sleeves
- [ ] narrow skirts
- [ ] thick or fuzzy bodice textures
- [ ] light values, brighter intensities

It may seem that men have far less to choose from than women do when planning a wardrobe. On the other hand, they also have far fewer chances for error! If men select classic styling in quality fabrics of complimentary colors, they can look good no matter what their body type.

For the most slimming effect, choose suits in dark or medium colors, in solids or narrow pin-stripes. Remember that a solid all-over color gives a longer, leaner appearance than pants and jacket in two different colors; this combination can draw attention to a bulging midsection.

Stick to a natural shoulder line with slight padding rather than a stiff, overstuffed look. Keep in mind that the body looks best when the shoulders appear wider than the hips. Jackets with a single back vent look slimmer than those with a double vent. A one or two button jacket is often a better choice than a double-breasted jacket, for it allows more shirt to

A beautiful tie can offer a chance for self-expression.

show and directs attention to the wearer's face.

Heavy men should beware of ill-fitting vests that gap around a problem waistline. In general, un-cuffed pants make the legs appear longer, and are a wise choice. Make sure the waistband is at the proper level; don't let it drop below the belly, or ride up above the natural waistline.

Men can draw attention toward the face by wearing a beautifully pressed white or pastel shirt in a high quality fabric. Make sure the shirt collar fits perfectly—not so tightly that the neck bulges. The shape of the collar should be flattering to the neck and face and should provide an attractive frame for the tie.

Neckwear should be of the highest affordable quality. A beautiful silk tie in a rich (not flamboyant) color becomes the focal point of the entire look. It is the one item in a man's wardrobe that offers a chance for self-expression. Select the width and length of the tie so that it flatters the wearer.

Proper Porportions

An aspect of design which is often overlooked when selecting fashions for men is the question of proportion. Men must keep all aspects of their clothing in proportion to their body size.

In other words, a small man looks best in a smaller collar, with average lapels and an average or narrow tie. Be certain that pants hems and sleeve cuffs are the proper length, neither too long nor too short. Short men should particularly be aware of the effect of a blazer and pants versus a suit in an all-over color.

Tall or big men also need to watch the proportion of their clothing; be sure that ties are long enough to end at the belt.

ABOUT KIDS

Children love color and clothes that are fun to look at and fun to wear. All of the tips in this book regarding design and construction of beautiful, wearable clothes for the disabled should be incorporated into thinking about kids' clothes. Be sure that the child you are making the outfit for is as much a part of the process as possible. Kids have strong likes and dislikes, and should let you know their needs and tastes. If you can, take them with you to local department stores and ask them which clothes they'd like to wear, what colors and details are most appealing. Take a sketch pad and make visual notes that you can refer to later on. You can also look at magazines with your child if that is easier. Then you can adapt a pattern to the aesthetic needs of your child as well as his or her functional needs.

Fabric stores, craft and hobby shops, and art supply stores are loaded with fabric paints, appliques, trimmings and decals to help make your child's clothes exciting to wear, no matter what the physical limitation. Most children love fashion and new trends. Remember that nothing affects a child's self-image as much as the clothing he or she wears!

A PORTFOLIO OF STYLES

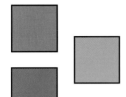

*These are three
hues of blue*

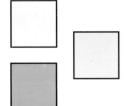

*These are three
intensities of blue*

Figure 2-1. The strong horizontal lines along
the yoke, waist and skirt hem make the
wearer appear shorter.

These are examples of warm colors

These are examples of cool colors

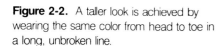

Figure 2-2. A taller look is achieved by wearing the same color from head to toe in a long, unbroken line.

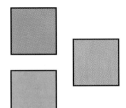

These neutral colors would give a soft effect

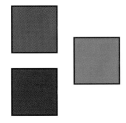

Dark colors help minimize the effect of bulky fabrics

Figure 2-3. Bright all-over color, bulky shapes and heavy fabrics can make a thin figure seem heavier.

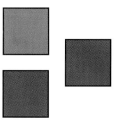

*Here are some
other color choices
for this outfit*

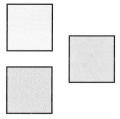

*Imagine the scarf
in one of these
accent colors*

Figure 2-4. Medium to dark color tones
and narrow vertical panels make the wearer
look thinner.

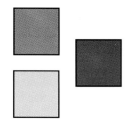

These warm colors would be other good choices for the dress

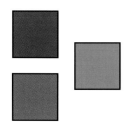

For some skin tones, cool colors are more flattering

Figure 2-5. To look thinner, add accents near the face and along vertical lines.

*Medium colors
and a dull surface
would be appropri-
ate for this blouse.*

*Pale colors and a
shiny texture are
not good choices
for this garment.*

Figure 2-6. A dowager's hump can be
camouflaged with front neck interest and
back bodice draping.

Picture this outfit in three shades of mauve.

Now picture three shades of blue.

Figure 2-7. The bustline can look smaller when the dress design includes a cowl neck and vertical stripes or tucks.

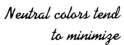

*Light colors can
be young and soft*

*Neutral colors tend
to minimize*

Figure 2-8. The illusion of a larger bust is achieved by adding a jabot neckline.

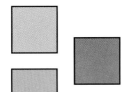

Happy colors lift the spirit.

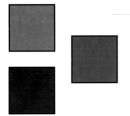

These drab colors may subdue our spirits.

Figure 2-9. A shoulder yoke and soft gathers give the appearance of a larger bust.

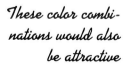

Figure 2-10. Make the waistline and abdomen look smaller by accenting the neckline and extending shoulders.

These color combinations would also be attractive

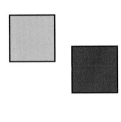

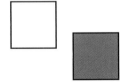

Other dominant and accent colors for the outfit shown.

Figure 2-11. A short double-breasted jacket will make the waistline look larger in a seated figure.

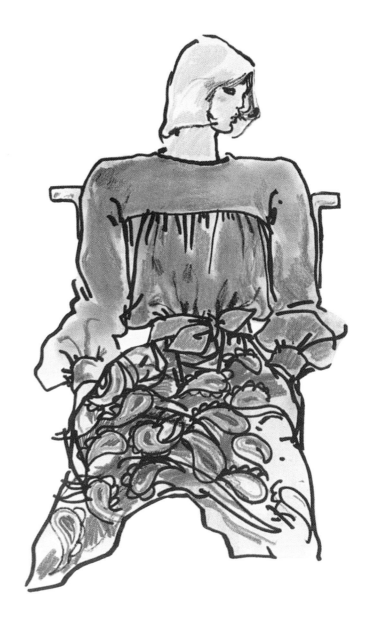

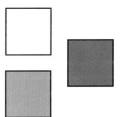

These neutrals would give a more subdued effect.

Here is another neutral color scheme.

Figure 2-12. Large-scale, brightly patterned skirts will make hips appear larger.

*These color combi-
nations would also
be attractive.*

Figure 2-13. A loosely-fitted jacket with
long, vertical lines will minimize the bustline.

A yellow raincoat with contrasting scarf is another option.

Bright colors are safest for rainwear.

Figure 2-14. Rainwear can be both pretty and practical when it is designed to protect the wearer while minimizing bulkiness in back.

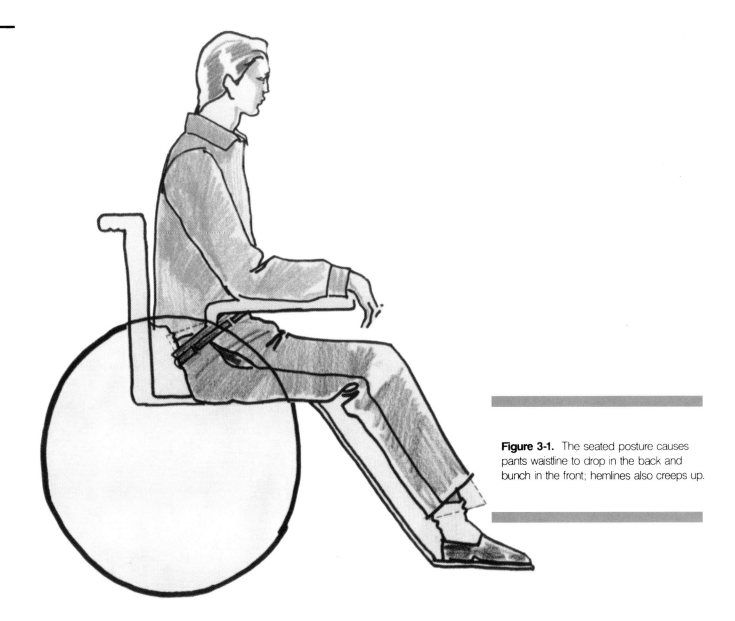

Figure 3-1. The seated posture causes pants waistline to drop in the back and bunch in the front; hemlines also creeps up.

Chapter 3

The Seated Figure

An estimated 20 million people in this country are confined to wheelchairs. This figure includes the physically disabled, the elderly, and the chronically ill. A large segment of each group spends a great part of each day in a seated position.

Poor fit affects the way clothing looks and feels. It is important to consider the physical changes in the sedentary body and to accommodate those particular changes when designing the garment. It is unreasonable to expect clothing to fit both an ambulatory person and a person in a wheelchair. These

It is important to consider body changes when designing for the seated figure.

35

Even if you are not disabled, think about the way your clothing feels after you have been sitting for several hours.

two very different body shapes require distinct solutions.

For good appearance, fit, and comfort, clothes must be designed specifically for the particular needs of a seated figure. Standard clothing is designed for the body in a standing position, which is different in many ways from the shape of a person who spends much of the time in a seated position. The body takes on an entirely new structure when seated, and clothing must accommodate and adapt to that shape in order be fashionable and functional.

FITTING CONSIDERATIONS

When we sit, the spine curves forward and stretches. This posture elongates the distance from the back of the waistline to the collar, causing the waistline of the garment to drop in the back. At the same time, the distance from the front of the waist to the neckline is reduced.

When standard clothing is designed, there is little concern for

Sedentary—a lifestyle which is mostly seated, with little activity.

Ambulatory—able to walk about.

Elongation—stretching or making longer.

Compression—pressing together, making shorter.

Ease—The amount of extra room in a garment which makes it comfortable to wear.

Ready-to-wear—clothing which is purchased, rather than custom made for the wearer.

Atrophy—weakening or wasting away of muscles.

Gusset—a small piece of fabric inserted into a seam to give more freedom of movement.

elongation and compression. When the wearer of the clothing is permanently sedentary, however, the pulling and bunching of fabric for a prolonged period of time will cause discomfort and these factors become more important.

If you are disabled, you know that special thought should be given to pants and skirts, as well as to shirts and blouses you would like to wear. If you are not disabled, consider for a moment what it is like sitting at a desk for a long period of time, or riding in a car

on a day-long trip, or even sitting in a movie theater throughout an epic film. Pants tend to tighten around the thighs and the crotch and cut into the skin. A rebellious sweater or shirttail may ride up and refuse to keep the lower back covered and clothing quickly becomes rumpled.

In addition to the changes in overall body shape, other factors affect comfort and appearance.

There is a change in girth as a person sits down. The body tends to spread, particularly in the

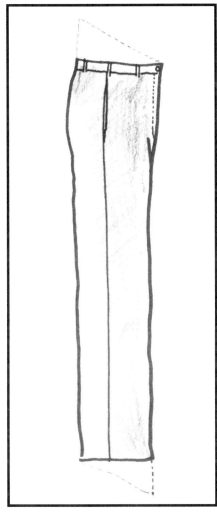

Figure 3-1b. Standard pants need adjustments at waist and hem to accommodate the seated figure.

thighs and buttocks. Extra room should be allowed in these areas of the garment. In most cases this extra ease can be incorporated into stylish, pleat-front pants. Knit fabrics will also make the pants more comfortable.

Another problem is that pants tend to ride up on the legs when the wearer is seated and the legs are bent. The pants length will look short, and excessive hosiery or bare legs will be exposed. The length from hip to ankle increases as the measurement is taken over the bent knee. For pants to fit properly a correction in inseam and outseam length must be made, as well as an adjustment along the pants hem that allows the front of the trouser to be longer than the back (see Fig. 3-1b). (Standard pants are often cut with the back longer than the front.)

PANTS FOR THE SEATED FIGURE

The following sections attempt to identify some of the primary concerns in designing pants for the seated figure. In each section, we will address a problem and present a variety of solutions and illustrations.

Making the Waistline Level

A pair of pants that fits well has a level waistline; that is, the waistline is equidistant from the floor in the back, front and sides. This creates a visually appealing waistline and a feeling of symmetry. As previously mentioned, the waistline in a seated figure drops considerably in the back. This downward pull is caused by the forward curve of the spine (see Figure 3-2).

In a clothed figure this change in position causes the fabric in the front of the pants to bunch up just below the waistline, unless it is specifically designed to do otherwise.

If you look at a seated person who is wearing pants, you will find rolls of material creating creases and unsightly bulges of fabric in the lower abdominal area and at

Pants patterns need several adjustments to fit the seated figure.

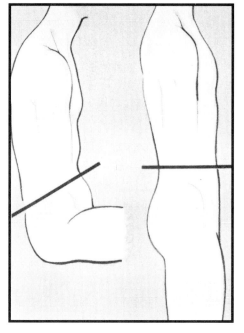

Figure 3-2a. *(left)* When the figure is seated the waistline slants down toward the back.

Figure 3-2b. *(right)* Unsightly creases and fabric bulges in the lap area are created when standard pants are worn by the seated figure.

A person with good basic sewing skills can adapt a pattern and create a visually appealing waistline.

the top of the legs. Although some bunching of fabric is important for a "normal" appearance and necessary when the seated person stands up, too much bulk is unsightly and can make the wearer feel constricted and self-conscious.

When a person wearing standard pants sits down, the waistline is not equidistant from the chair all the way around the body. Instead, there is slant from the front to the back of the body. Ideally all points of the waistline should be the same level from the floor. This rule is true whether the person is standing or seated.

A person with good sewing skills can adapt any trouser pattern and create a visually appealing waistline. Step-by-step directions for doing this are given in Chapter 6. The flat pattern will have an oval waistline which is extremely high in the back and low in the front. After waistline adjustments have been made, pants for the sedentary figure will have no unsightly fabric folds in the lap area and sloppy shirttails will stay tucked in. The wearer will look well groomed, with an appearance that is difficult to achieve using ready-to-wear pants. The wearer will also be more comfortable, as the pants

Figure 3-16. The ready-to-wear jacket cannot accommodate the shape changes in the seated figure.

Figure 3-17. Adjustments made to the front of the jacket will give the sedentary businessman a professional fit.

Alteration of the jacket pattern can eliminate many problems.

they are enlarged at the hipline to accommodate increased girth. A smooth line can be maintained from the front of the jacket around to the shortened back, effecting a "normal" appearance.

In summary, the problems most evident in a standard jacket or coat worn by a seated figure are:

- gaping at lapel line (see Figures 3-14—3-17)

- upper shoulder area too narrow

- neckline and collarline too high in back

- armhole too high

- hipline too narrow

- hemline too long in front and back

- sleeves not contoured for a bent arm

- sleeve hem too short

Chapter 6 will provide instructions for altering standard jacket patterns to eliminate these problems.

Women have a certain advantage in clothing that men do not. Men's clothing is more uniform in appearance; the businessman's jacket must be of a certain length and shape to look appropriate. A professional woman, on the other hand, can wear jackets in varying lengths and styles, yet still look businesslike.

A seated woman's best option is simply to select a jacket that ends at hip-level (see Figure 3-18). In this way a very smooth, tailored look is possible and the length problem is avoided.

SHIRTS & BLOUSES

The fundamental concern when selecting or designing shirts or blouses for the seated figure is comfort. They should not bind around the neckline, armhole, hips, or abdomen. The most functional solution is to choose a blouse and skirt rather than a dress. Selecting a two-piece outfit gives the wearer the additional advantage of playing one garment against the other for contrast in color, shape, and texture.

Figure 3-18. A hip-length jacket gives the sedentary figure a smooth look.

High collars on shirts, blouses and sweaters tend to ride up when the wearer is seated and should be avoided. A better choice might be a collarless blouse accessorized with a bright scarf or interesting necklace. Aesthetically, a skirt worn with an overblouse or tunic is appealing. If the skirt is a dark color and the blouse light, a large abdomen and other fitting problems in the lap area can be camouflaged.

Commercially manufactured shirts do not usually pose much of a fitting problem if the fabric is soft enough to mold to the extremes of body contour. Sleeve length should be slightly longer to accommodate bent elbows and the

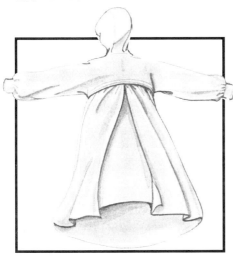

Figure 3-19. This raincoat design features an inner panel at center back for protection from the rain. The slit outer layer can be pulled aside for comfortable sitting.

raglan or kimono sleeve, whether in a jacket or blouse, provides the most freedom of movement.

It is best to choose garments which open in the front or side. As a general guide, necklines should be loose enough to be comfortable and sleeves should be cut on the full side. Clothing for those who cannot dress by themselves may open in the back to make the dresser's job easier. Make sure that the back opening does not have thick buttons or other fasteners which may make the garment uncomfortable for the person to wear when sitting.

OUTERWEAR & RAINWEAR

Avoid bulkiness when constructing outerwear. Coats have a large quantity of excess fabric that must be stuffed into the wheelchair behind and around the wearer. This fabric is in constant danger of being caught in the wheels of the chair itself. Many wheelchair-bound individuals prefer short jackets for this reason.

Of course, a coat provides much more warmth and coverage in the lap and lower body. Try to design a garment which provides warmth and protection without excess fabric.

The ideal garment for rain or cold is one that is shorter in back than in front. It can be slit down the center back so the wearer does not have to sit on many folds of fabric. Capes which are shorter in the back are often a good choice. The wearer merely pulls the fabric away and arranges it around the body rather than tucking it under. It is helpful if the sleeves have inner liners that are elasticized at the wrist to keep cold and moisture out. The wheelchair-bound person is somewhat vulnerable to accidents in that he or she is half the height of the standing figure. Yellow or other light, bright colors or reflective bands make the wearer more visible and add to safety as well as providing an emotional lift.

Shirts and blouses should be comfortable, attractive and easy to put on.

will not constrict or bind at the waist.

The physical condition of the individual may cause difficulties in fitting. It is quite common for sedentary people to gain excess weight in the midsection. Lack of exercise causes the muscles to lose tone and the abdominal area to spread. The increased abdominal size is emphasized when ill-fitting pants bunch in the lap area. This excess fabric draws further attention to the sagging muscle tissue— a situation which may give the disabled individual a negative self-concept.

One way to correct the problem is to use a commercially-available wide, nonslip waistband stiffener. Certain ready-to-wear pants feature this three- to four-inch rubberized reinforcement at the waist to provide a smoother look for the able-bodied and to help shirttails remain tucked in. The same reinforcement can be used for the disabled seated person as a form of "girdle" to help control sagging muscle tissue and smooth out the garment line. You

can also attach loops at each side of the waistband to help the person pull the pants on. These remedies will provide the wearer with more support, better appearance, and, it is hoped, a better self-image.

The Pocket Problem

The pockets in the average ready-to-wear pair of pants, whether located in the back or front of the pants, are often totally inaccessible to the wheelchair-bound person. The seated posture causes the pocket area to buckle and be drawn tautly around the hips, making entry of a hand difficult if not impossible (see Figure 3-3). These pockets are not only useless, they also produce unsightly and uncomfortable bulges and ridges.

The intensity of this problem was observed by the Design Without Limits (DWL) group when a wheelchair-bound man struggled to reach the keys in his right front pants pocket. He tried to lift his right hip off the chair by leaning all of his upper body weight over

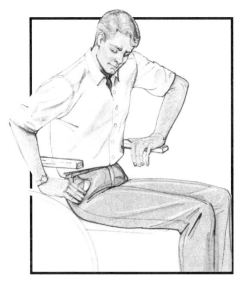

Figure 3-3. The sedentary person has great difficulty using traditional pants pockets.

all of his upper body weight over the left hip. His armless wheelchair gave him no support as he leaned over and tried to balance himself on his left hip by using his left hand as a wedge between his body and the chair. Simultaneously, he tried to pry his other hand into the pocket which was drawn tightly around his abdomen. By the time he pulled his keys free, he was perspiring heavily. Many persons with lower body immobility are not able to go through the

Loops placed at each side of the waistband can make it easier to pull the pants on.

contortions that this man did to reach in a pocket.

The simplest solution to the entire pocket dilemma is to eliminate them altogether. This may not always be feasible, since everyone needs to carry belongings in a secure place.

When designing a workable pocket, there are several factors one must consider. The angle of pocket placement is very important. In other words, the pocket must be located in direct line with the hand that uses that pocket. For the seated person, that line begins below the hipbone and follows down toward the thigh and knee. The hand of a seated person can most easily enter a pocket if that pocket is placed in the thigh area rather than at the hip.

The shape of the pocket must accommodate the size and shape of the hand. A pocket should not be so small that the wearer has to squeeze his hand into it. It should not be so large that it detracts from the overall aesthetic of the pants.

Finally, there are the issues of

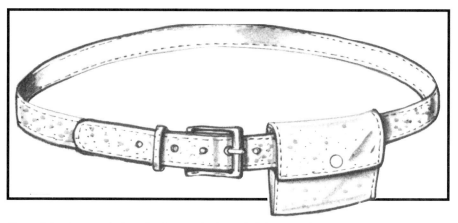

Figure 3-4. A purse designed to be attached to a belt is a good alternative for carrying valuables.

security and location of pocket opening. Gravity has a way of helping the contents of a pocket fall out if the opening is carelessly placed. Usually, a pocket with a top opening rather than a side opening is best. A flapped and buttoned pocket, a pocket closed with hook and loop tape, or a zippered pocket will help to keep contents secure if the wearer can operate the fastening.

Some disabled persons use a container such as a tote bag that hangs from the back or arms of a wheelchair instead of a pocket. However, these containers don't

provide security for carrying valuables and can appear cluttered or unprofessional. Purses or wallets made of fine leather can be attached or buckled onto a belt or belt carrier. These can add a quality look to individual appearance rather than detract from it (see Figure 3-4).

Casual pants, such as sport slacks or jeans, can easily be designed to include functional pockets. These pants are not intended for business dress and can therefore feature accessible patch pockets.

A pocket for denim jeans that

has received positive feedback from wheelchair-bound people was designed as a double-decker pocket stitched on to the thigh area of the pants. The bottom part of the pocket is open on one side; the top (see Figure 3-5) of the twin pocket, which securely holds contents and provides design interest, is closed with a zipper.

In addition to being accessible and functional, there is another particular advantage to locating of the pocket at the thigh. When a person leans forward in a wheelchair, there is often a loss of balance and a fear of toppling over. Putting the hands into these deep patch pockets helps to stabilize the weight on the chair and allows a greater feeling of security (see Figure 3-6).

A pair of standard dress pants, or business attire, requires a differ-ent solution to the pocket problem. Since the wearer probably wishes to look businesslike, a patch pocket on the front of wool gabardine trousers is inappropriate. A useful option is to enclose long, invisible, vertical pockets within the outseam of the pants from the top of the thigh down to the knee. Some disabled persons prefer this type of pocket enclosed within the inseam rather than the outseam. This is acceptable as long as the

Choose pocket styles which complement the design of the garment.

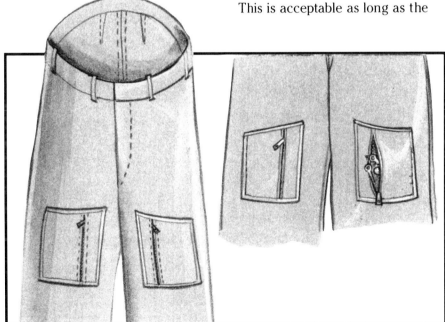

Figure 3-5. The double-decker pocket is accessible and functional.

pocket does not interfere with accessibility to the collection bag in the case of incontinence (see Figure 3-7).

The pocket is a very important consideration for the

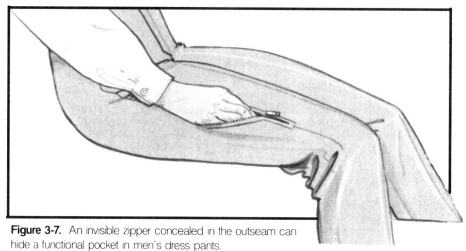

Figure 3-7. An invisible zipper concealed in the outseam can hide a functional pocket in men's dress pants.

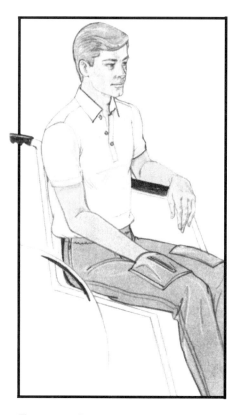

Figure 3-6. Pockets located on the thigh can provide a feeling of stability.

wheelchair-bound individual. A safe, secure carrying space for valuables should be provided as part of garment construction, with accessibility as a primary design concern.

Front Opening Adjustments

Because pants designed for the seated figure must be cut substantially lower in the front than in the back, the length of the fly becomes much shorter. Even though the front opening is reduced greatly, it must be included in the garment design. If the fly in men's pants is to be used for personal needs, the opening must extend farther down along the crotch seam than in traditional pants. In this instance the zipper should be of the very lightweight and flexible variety, preferably the nylon version.

Appearance and attention to a man's self-image requires that the fly be constructed for a look and feeling of "normalcy." Sometimes a

Chapter 4

The Standing Figure

At first glance, the wheel-chair-bound individual presents a very calm, composed picture. This is, of course, due to his or her seated position. Because such people cannot move about in a "normal" fashion, we tend to see them as quiet and immobile.

The crutch-bound person seems to make quite the opposite presentation. He or she is often observed as a dishevelled, askew victim, struggling to maintain stability as well as a tidy physical appearance. The effort necessary to walk using crutches or braces is

Persons using crutches have special clothing needs.

Figure 4-1. A person on crutches can often have a disheveled appearance caused by the extremes in body movement required for walking.

often so intense that attention to one's clothing can be overlooked. Clothes that fit and are adapted properly can go a long way toward improving the appearance of the person who uses crutches.

Imagine, for a moment, an individual on crutches. His or her pants are probably sliding down, shirttails are pulling out, jackets are hiked up under the arms and the jacket front stands away from the body (see Figure 4-1).

These problems are created by the extremes in body movement required for walking. They cannot be eliminated entirely, but design adaptations can offer some aid.

In this chapter we will discuss various types of clothing and their relationship to the use of braces, prostheses and crutches. You should bear in mind throughout the discussion whether or not the clothing itself prohibits or enhances movements specific to these devices and whether or not the clothing disguises or draws attention to them.

DESIGNING PANTS AND SKIRTS

For the individual who wears a prosthesis or brace, pants can serve as a form of camouflage. Pants should be cut wide enough in the leg to fall smoothly over and around the assistive device without drawing attention to the problem area. When considering appropriate camouflage, fabric is a primary concern and a medium to heavy weight, non-clingy cloth should be selected. If you prefer knits, beware of clingy fabrics and opt for a heavy, double knit if possible. Dark colors are a good choice, as they tend to be more opaque than lighter shades. Smooth surfaced fabrics slide over a brace or prosthesis more easily than do rough textures such as corduroy. Therefore, they are more comfortable and easier to put on. A zipper may be inserted along the inseam of the appropriate leg to provide access to the brace.

Other points to consider in making pants easy to put on include:

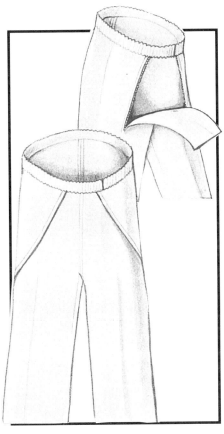

Figure 4-2. Flap-front pants are easy to put on and provide easier personal care.

- Fly fronts with low openings help pants to slide on and off easily.
- Flap front pants with a waistband that hold the back on while the front is being adjusted (see Figure 4-2) can be helpful.
- Pants should be cut slightly on the wide side in the leg area so they are easier to put on and take off. They should not be so wide as to catch in the crutches or present an unusual appearance.
- One of the most helpful dressing features is a set of good, sturdy belt loops on every pair of pants. These enable the wearer to slip his or her fingers or a dressing hook through the loops to pull the pants up.

Other Issues

Wear and tear on the garment caused by the abrasiveness of the appliance is often a problem. The constant stress the device places on the fabric makes holes appear in that one area although the re-

mainder of the garment is still completely intact. To avoid this problem, pants should be lined and reinforced whenever possible. You can do this by stitching a separate layer or layers of fabric into the seams of the pants or by using an iron-on patch (nylon is the strongest) in the appropriate area. For the best appearance, all of this "patchwork" should be done on the inside of the garment. Pants may also be fully lined, with the reinforcement sewn into the lining only. As a result, the lining can be repaired repeatedly without damage to the outer garment.

An interesting and functional alternative design idea was created by DWL in the form of zip-off pants (see Figure 4-3). A separating zipper was incorporated into the design horizontally around the thigh to accommodate a lower-leg prosthesis. The entire portion of the pants below mid-thigh can then be replaced when the fabric begins to wear. In addition, these pants serve a dual function as either shorts or full-length trousers. A necessary feature in the

Reinforce the inside of pants for added durability.

For crutch users, suspenders may be preferable to a belt.

construction of the pants is a flap of fabric sewn under the zipper to protect the skin from contact with the zipper teeth when the pants are worn full-length. When worn as shorts, this flap of fabric is turned up to become a cuff and conceal the zipper teeth completely.

Crutches do not strain or rub the fabric of trousers. They do, however, elongate the body because of the stretching motion used in walking. You must be sure the waistline fits securely so the pants don't slide down the body when in motion. Using snug-fitting elastic (either all the way around the waistline or just in the back) is helpful since this elastic will expand and contract with the movement of the wearer. Both men and women may find suspenders preferable to a belt. Women who use crutches should be concerned that their skirts are not so full as to get in the way of the crutches.

Issues affecting individuals who are temporarily disabled and must wear a cast are much the same as those affecting others

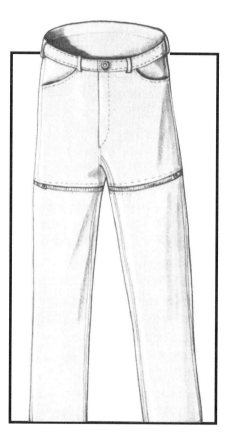

Figure 4-3. Zip-off pants are a functional design for prosthesis wearers.

who wear appliances. Here, however, temporary garment adjustments can be made such as opening a side seam and stitching in a gusset or inverted pleat which can later be removed and the seam rejoined.

The problem of incontinence can be handled in much the same way as for the wheelchair-bound person. Zippers stitched into the inseams of a pant leg can make the collection bag more accessible. Dark colored fabrics are again helpful, as are wraparound garments for women.

UPPER TORSO ACCOMMODATIONS

When an individual must use crutches, body movements become greatly exaggerated. This is especially true in terms of motion in the upper part of the body. For the person on crutches, most of the muscle activity required for walking takes place from the waist up. This, then, plays havoc on the clothing in this area.

As described earlier, garments bunch up under the arms around the crutches, hemlines of shirts and tops rise up and are pulled out from pants and skirts, and great stress is placed on all the construction lines within the garment.

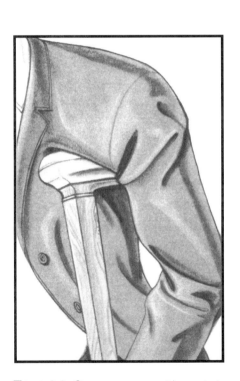

Figure 4-4. Stress on a garment is greatest at the underarm when the wearer uses crutches.

Stresses and Strains

For the person on crutches, the underarm where the crutch makes contact with the body may create the greatest problems (see Figure 4-4). If the crutch used is the type with a forearm cuff, the sleeve of the garment then becomes the problem area. For both types of crutches, sleeves should be cut long enough so that they don't rise up too far on the arm when the crutch is moved. In both cases, the area across the shoulder blades in put under constant stress; there is a tendency toward ripping the seams apart at the armhole. At least three to four inches of extra ease should be built into the garment to relieve this problem. You can provide a release pleat or flange at the armhole. Directions for changing your pattern are included in Chapter 6. This method assures that the jacket or top will look neat and fit well when the wearer is not moving and still allow for freedom of movement when required (see Figure 4-5).

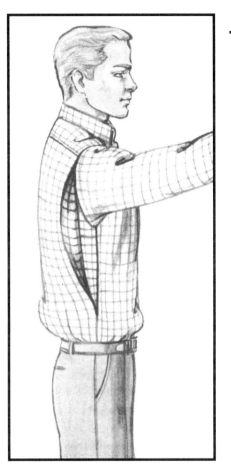

Figure 4-5. A release pleat at the armhole allows for freedom of movement for the person on crutches.

Release pleats and gussets may be added to ready-to-wear shirts and jackets.

Choose a sleeve style which is comfortable and flattering.

As to sleeves, the notion that a lower, more widely scooped armhole allows more freedom is false. The truth of the matter is that the higher the armhole the greater the freedom of movement. This point should only be taken to reasonable limits, however, and an armhole should not be cut so high that it is uncomfortable to the underarm, causing friction against the skin.

The most functional sleeves for crutch and even wheelchair users (propelling a wheelchair requires extra arm movement similar to using crutches) are kimono or raglan sleeve (see Figure 4-6). These allow for greater freedom of movement because they are cut larger and squarer, and less stress is placed on a single seam. When this type of sleeve is inappropriate (as it often is for a man) a gusset can be set into the underarm area of a standard sleeve (see Figure 4-7). These diamond-shaped insets can also allow much freedom of movement while decreasing stress on seam lines.

Another option is to reinforce the underarm area either by stitch-

Prosthesis—an artificial body part; in this instance, an artificial limb.

Dressing Hook—a large, easily-grasped hook which enables a person with limited mobility to pull on clothing.

Kimono Sleeve—A wide, straight sleeve which is set into a deep, square armhole.

Raglan sleeve—a sleeve which has a long slanting seam from neck to armhole, such as in a sweatshirt.

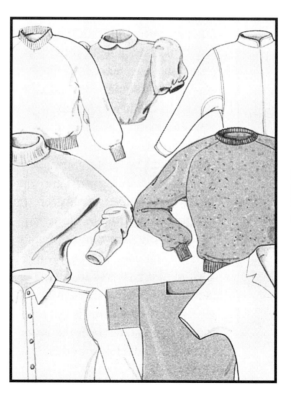

Figure 4-6. The type of sleeve used in any garment design dictates the amount of freedom of movement the wearer will have.

Figure 4-7. A gusset set into the underarm of a standard shirt provides a great deal of freedom of movement.

ing seam tape along the seam lines (from the inside) or by constructing the garment with the flat-felled seams used in jeans (See Figure 4-8). This type of construction technique will help as far as stress on the fabric is concerned but will not aid in providing extra comfort. In addition, an extra layer of self-fabric or nylon patch can be stitched on the inside of the garment to help retain its shape and strength.

Whenever possible, the individual who uses crutches should choose an overblouse or sweater worn on the outside of pants or skirt. This is a better fashion alternative than wearing a shirt that refuses to stay tucked in. If, however, the shirt must be tucked in, it should be cut longer that usual (a good four inches is best). Men may wish to consider the option of buttons sewn to the shirttail, with but-

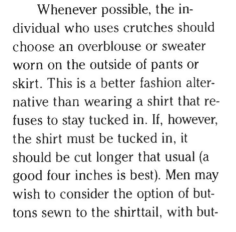

Figure 4-8. Seam tape applied along the underarm will eliminate stress on the fabric created by crutches.

tonhole tabs or loops attached inside the trouser waistband. Women might choose a bodysuit or blouse with attached panties.

Pockets on all garments should be large, loose, and well-placed, so that they are functional for the individual with imperfect balance. That is, they must be easy to reach if the wearer must let go of one crutch and balance with a single arm. They must allow quick exit and entry of the hand. Finally they should offer a good deal of security. The individual who needs both arms to hold up his crutches cannot be worried that the contents of his pockets are vulnerable. The solution is for the pockets to be closed by a zipper or by a flap secured with hook and loop tape.

OVERALL APPEARANCE

The design considerations that are important to the ambulatory disabled do not vary too much from those for the average non-disabled person. The individual's features must be objectively as-

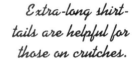

Extra-long shirt-tails are helpful for those on crutches.

Figure 4-9. A person who walks using crutches tends to pull his or her clothing out of position with each motion.

sessed, the positive ones accented and the negative ones downplayed. Height, weight, and coloring all come into play. As mentioned earlier, the person whose rhythm of movement is not smooth tends to pull his or her clothing out of position with each motion. Pants or a skirt worn with a sweater or overblouse allow each segment individual movement. This is much more flattering than trying to wear a tucked-in shirt that pulls away from the trousers or skirt. Fabrics with some degree of stretch or elasticity are more flattering and comfortable than stiff woven fabric because they "give" with the exaggerated movements of the wearer.

For a man or woman with spinal deformity such as scoliosis, the pattern of the fabric can either create an illusion of symmetry or draw attention to the irregularity. For instance, if the fabric pattern that is chosen is a horizontal stripe, the disability will be greatly emphasized (see Figure 4-10). A large non-repetitive print would be much more appropriate.

Figure 4-10. A horizontal stripe emphasizes the figure irregularities of the individual with scoliosis; a better solution on the right disguises the problem.

It is nearly impossible to alter ready-to-wear clothing to fit this particular disability. One shoulder is noticeably lower than the other and the alternate hip is much higher. Therefore, garments must be designed specifically for this inequality. You must reshape the shoulder and hipline during the pattern-alteration stage. (Patternmaking for this specific problem is discussed in Chapter 6).

Chapter 5

Issues of Limited Dexterity

The art of dressing and un-dressing ourselves requires coordination of sight, sensation, dexterity, balance, and muscular strength. Since many physical disabilities limit coordination, the ability to dress oneself may be severely limited. Pain, fatigue, fear, agitation, and frustration also add to the individual's inability to perform motions we often take for granted. Often the seemingly simple task of pulling on one's pants is a time-consuming, exhausting task for a disabled person (see Figure 5-1).

Ease of dressing and undressing is important when choosing clothing for the disabled.

61

Inability to dress and undress can rob a disabled person of feelings of self-worth.

Dexterity—skill in using the body, or parts of the body.

Separating Zipper—a sportswear zipper with two pulls which can be unzipped from top or bottom; often used on ski jackets and pants.

Halo Brace—a circular brace which is anchored to the patient's skull and then fastened to a shoulder harness; used in treatment of neck and spinal fractures.

Flange—an insert set into the shoulder seam of a garment to provide greater mobility.

Dependent Dressing—dressing which must be assisted or even performed completely by another person.

Independent Dressing—the ability to dress oneself.

If specialized clothing for the disabled were presented at the rehabilitative level, much of the frustration and negative self-concept could be minimized.

The inability to dress and undress can rob a disabled individual of necessary feelings of satisfaction, pride, and self-worth. And even though fit, color, and comfort are important features to consider in the design of a garment, the problem of ease in dressing and undressing is often of greatest importance. Therefore, the issues concerning limited dexterity will be examined in this chapter.

This section will be divided into three areas: restricted arm dexterity, which results in limited arm motions; limited finger dexterity, having to do with finely-tuned movements such as buttoning or zipping; and dependent dressing, when the individual requires aid from another person in order to be dressed.

Most rehabilitation hospitals train disabled people to dress themselves, if their particular weaknesses allow these skills to be developed. However, they are often taught to dress themselves using clothes they had before becoming disabled. This is a highly frustrating experience for the disabled person because the old clothing has none of the design features required to simplify dressing.

Pulling on an extra-large knit shirt by first getting the arms through and then pulling the shirt over the head is often accomplished with difficulty even though the size of the shirt, the large armholes and the stretch of the knit fabric actually simplify the process. Putting on a man's dress shirt with its high armholes, narrow sleeves and endless buttons is often impossible to accomplish independently.

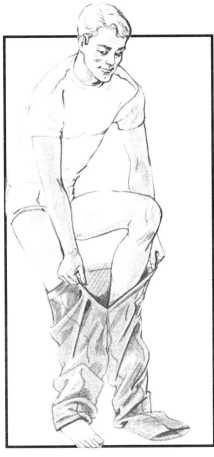

Figure 5-1. Putting pants on can be a time-consuming and exhausting task for a disabled person.

RESTRICTED ARM DEXTERITY

The term "arm dexterity" can be defined as the movements required by the upper arm and shoulders to enable a person to put on and take off clothing. To put on a jacket, for instance, the garment must be held in one hand while the other arm is inserted into a sleeve. Then the jacket must be maneuvered around the back of the body and the other arm inserted (see Figure 5-2). The entire upper body is used in this process.

Figure 5-2. Restricted arm dexterity can make putting on a jacket very difficult.

The notion of slipping clothing on over the head is a difficult one and should only be attempted with sportswear in stretchy fabrics. Golf shirts, for instance, in cotton interlock with a tab front closing are a possibility, but most other types of slip-on clothing should be avoided. High collars, especially turtlenecks, are very difficult to pull on. Full slips can also be a problem. The best option is to select styles that have a center front closing either all the way down the front or at least two-thirds of the way.

Avoid garments which must be pulled on over the head.

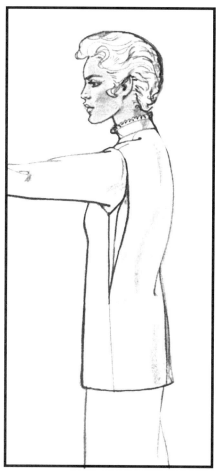

Figure 5-3. Flanges along the armhole of a jacket can make it much easier to put on.

Problems with Jackets and Coats

For those with fairly good control of the upper body, a coat or jacket can be put on without too much stress if the back is cut wide enough and the armholes are not restrictively high. The sleeve that is most practical, not just for putting on but also for comfort and ease of movement, is the raglan or the kimono sleeve. A man's tailored sport coat would not allow such liberty, but if a design choice among various sleeve types can be made, choose an alternative to the normal set-in sleeve. Pleats and flanges in the back of garments and in the armhole area are also very helpful (see Figure 5-3).

If mobility is severely limited, it may be necessary to apply zippers in the underarm and side seam area. Sometimes two zippers are used (keep them of the soft, lightweight variety), one from the underarm to wrist and the other from underarm to hem. This solution allows the jacket to be put on with very little twisting of the up-

Figure 5-4. Double ended zippers applied along the underarm and side seams are helpful when mobility is severely limited.

per body. The individual may, however, need some help with zipping the seams closed (see Figure 5-4).

An exception to this rule is the poncho or cape for inclement weather. These garments often have no sleeves and slip over the head with minimal effort.

Problems with Trousers

The disabled person who has limited movement of the upper

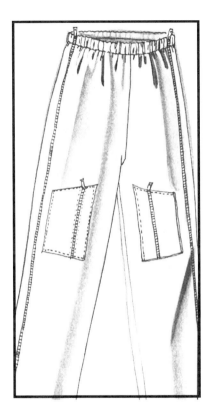

Figure 5-5. Double ended zippers along the outseam of pants can help with dependent dressing.

spine has great difficulty putting on trousers as well. Indeed, special design features must be built into not only jackets, but virtually all of the clothing he or she wears.

Most wheelchair-bound persons must lie down to put on their pants. Very often the fly opening alone does not allow sufficient room for the hips to slide through. You can remedy this problem by inserting long separating zippers down the side seams of the pants. Another option is creating drop-front pants much like those used by the U.S. Navy (see Chapter 3). In these cases, an elastic waistband can be used to hold the pants up while the front section is being adjusted. Side-zipped or drop front pants also make personal care easier for such persons (see Figure 5-5).

Interestingly, a DWL participant noticed that pants with the high-in-the-back, low-in-the-front waistline caused less difficulty in dressing than did regular pants. He did not require the use of side zippers or a drop front.

Another feature that is extremely helpful in donning trousers are good, sturdy belt loops; these are an invaluable aid to pulling the pants on.

RESTRICTED FINGER DEXTERITY

For those with limited dexterity, one of the greatest difficulties in the process of dressing and undressing is reaching and using fastenings. One way to deal with this problem is to eliminate as many fastenings as possible, and to use pull-on or wraparound garments. This solution might work well for people whose fingers don't function well but who are able to perform larger bodily movement. If, however, an individual can neither slip a shirt on over his or her head nor cope with the buttons, further adaptations are necessary.

Some Useful Fasteners

The material that has served as the most functional closing for garments for individuals with hand

Small fasteners can create problems for those with limited finger dexterity.

Hook and loop tape can replace buttons or other fasteners.

dexterity problems is hook and loop tape. Velcro™ is one such tape.

This fastener is a combination of hook tape and loop tape that locks together with a slight touch. It is available in various widths and pre-cut shapes. The tape can be used instead of buttons, hooks and eyes or snaps, and is a saving grace for the individual who has difficulty maneuvering small closures. Hook and loop tape can be used in combination with buttons for a shirt front. Remove the buttons and sew small squares of loop tape where the buttons were. Sew the buttons (now simply decorative) on the outside of the buttonhole placket, centering each button on a buttonhole. Complete the alteration by sewing small matching squares of hook tape to the underside of the buttonholes. The shirt will now have the appearance of a conventionally buttoned garment, but little dexterity will be required to close the placket.

The disadvantages in the use of hook and loop tape lie in the fact that it can be very irritating if

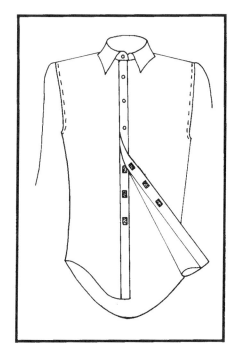

Figure 5-6. Small squares of hook and loop tape can substitute for buttons on a shirt or blouse.

it rubs against the skin. In addition, if the opened tape sections come in contact with other fabrics during laundering, snagging can result.

If the tape is overused it can become synonymous with a "handicapped garment." Care should be taken to make the tape inconspicuous and the sections used should only be large enough to keep the garment closed securely. In other words, avoid the use of long, continuous strips in any one area. Used carefully and in small amounts, however, it can provide functional qualities without detracting from overall appearance.

Other Fasteners

For the most part, hook and loop tape and zippers with large pulls seem to be the best closures for the person with limited finger dexterity. It has been found that among the most difficult fasteners to maneuver are small buttons, hooks and eyes, snaps, and prong buckles. Once you are aware of the pitfalls, you can find workable solutions.

Large buttons, at least the size of a nickel, should be used if buttons are used at all. Small buttons are difficult to handle but the illusion of a buttoned garment can often be maintained. Another helpful point to note is that any button is more maneuverable if it has a metal or thread shank at its base so the button stands away from the fabric. This makes the button easier to grasp.

Buttons can be sewn on with elastic thread, especially on cuffs, so they don't have to be unbuttoned to let the hand pass in and out. Buttonholes should be large enough to allow the button to slip through easily. The button loop and toggle are easier to fasten than the button and buttonhole.

Other closings to consider are zippers and hooks. Zippers should have large pulls or tabs which are easy to grasp. These can add a decorative element to a jacket or vest as well as make opening and closing easier. Large metal hooks on skirts and pants are easier to maneuver than small snaps or hooks and eyes. The latter should be avoided in practically all cases.

One new development in closures that is being researched by DWL is the magnetic fastener. It is extremely functional and has thus far been used in belts and heavy outerwear.

Before applying any fastener, note that the particular limitations of the individual must be analyzed in association with the design of the garment. What is functional for one person may be a problem for another.

DEPENDENT DRESSING

The term "dependent dressing" is used here in reference to the individual who requires assistance in dressing and undressing. In this situation clothing must be designed to appeal on an aesthetic level to the person wearing the garment but it must also be designed with consideration for the person doing the dressing. It is extremely difficult to support the body weight of an immobile individual and very uncomfortable and often painful for that individual to be manhandled and forced into a garment.

Based on studies done by DWL in conjunction with patients who were not able to provide any assistance in their own dressing, certain conclusions were drawn. It was easiest for the dresser and the dressee if lower body garments (pants, underwear, etc.) could open out flat on a bed and then the patient could lie down to be dressed. In this case, the pants used had double-ended separating zippers in each side seam so they could be zipped closed after the patient was in them. These pants had an extra advantage in that diapering these patients was made easier.

If side seam zippers are not used it is helpful if the garment fabric has some stretch quality to it

New fasteners are being developed which are easier to use.

and if the waistband is elasticized. Men's dress trousers, however, don't always provide these features and may present problems. In this case the fly can be lowered enough to make the waistline wide enough for a roomy entry.

Shirts and jackets can also be designed for easy entry. The garments should preferably open all the way down the front or back rather than be of the pull-on variety. In the case of a severely immobile or heavy person, the shirt or jacket can be opened down both the front and the back. Then the dresser need only slip the person's arms through the sleeves and close the front and back. This styling is also very useful for the person who must wear a halo brace.

It is important to remember that there is a great difference between the incapacitated person who cannot lift arms or legs, the arthritic person who cannot button his shirt, and the severely disabled person who can't help himself dress at all. Each problem requires a unique design solution and should be treated accordingly.

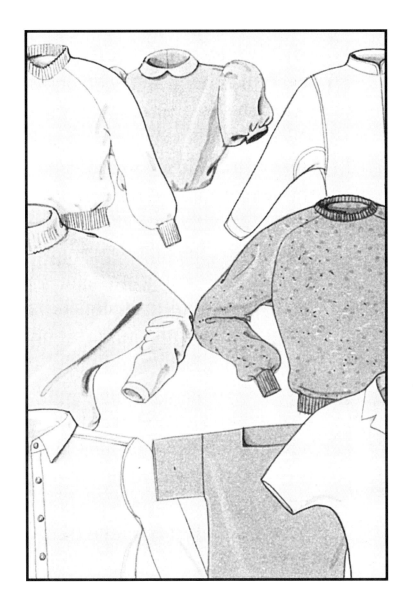

Chapter 6

Measurements, Patterns, Fabrication

This chapter is designed to aid the experienced seamstress or tailor. There is not the time or space in this publication to devote to the elementary issues of pattern-making and garment construction. Refer to books on the reading list (pages 94–95) to learn about sewing basics. The designer must evaluate the person's needs and select a pattern and a fabric that answers those needs as closely as possible. You should have a clear understanding of the

*Measurements
must be taken
while the person
maintains his or
her normal
posture.*

functional and aesthetic needs of the individual for whom the clothing is being made. Design principles as well as an awareness of the subject's physical and emotional concerns should be taken into account. Some points to consider include:

- Do the design lines and fabric mask the disability or draw attention to it?

- Are the design lines placed with regard to the stress the garment will receive from extremes in body movement?

- Is the proportion, shape, and color flattering to the wearer?

- Is comfort taken well into account when selecting the design and fabric?

- Is the garment designed for convenient dressing and undressing?

After you've reached a decision regarding garment design, you must adjust the pattern to the wearer's measurements and disabilities. One of the most important

---

True the line—To re-draw the edge of a pattern piece so that a smooth line or curve is achieved.

Bodice—A blouse or the upper part of a dress.

Medium—The material in which an artist works (such as clay, paint, video or fabric).

Synthetic—A man-made fiber (rather than one which occurs naturally) such as nylon, acetate, polyester, etc.

---

considerations is that these measurements be taken while the subject maintains his normal stance. In other words, if the individual spends most of his time seated in a wheelchair, the measurements should be taken while he is in that position. This is necessary because the body's dimensions change drastically as the stance of the body changes. Some of the measurements taken will be new to even the experienced sewer because critical points also change in relation to position. For example, for the wheelchair-bound person, the crotch length measurement is critical. Therefore a measurement must be taken from the center of the crotch up to the waist in the back and also in the front.

An illustrated description of necessary measurements follows and a chart is included into which these dimensions can be entered. It is very difficult and tiring to take measurements of the seated figure. Measure slowly, methodically and as accurately as possible. If braces or a prosthesis are worn, measurements must be taken with the devices in place.

MEASUREMENT GUIDELINES

These measurements are taken, not with an eye to drafting original patterns from scratch, but to altering commercially-made patterns to fit the disabled person. A high degree of skill is

MEASUREMENT TIPS

↙ Don't try to take your own measurements by yourself. Only a contortionist can do it success-fully! Enlist the aid of a friend.

↙ For women and girls, take the measurements over undergar-ments or a leotard. For men and boys, take them over a T-shirt and shorts or unbelted, light-weight slacks.

↙ Stand in a relaxed position (or sit, if that is your normal position) and look straight ahead.

↙ To locate the natural waistline, tie a string snugly around the waist. If the waist is hard to find (a common problem on men and children), have them bend side-ways. The crease that forms is at the natural waistline.

↙ To find the shoulder point, raise the arm to shoulder level. A dim-ple will form at the shoulder bone—that is the shoulder point.

↙ To find the back neck bone, bend the head forward so you can feel the first neck bone, or vertebra.

↙ To locate the base of the neck in front, shrug your shoulders so that a hollow forms at the neck base.

↙ For the "around" measurments, keep the tape measure parallel to the floor. The tape should be snug, but not tight, against your body.

↙ Retake these measurements every six months, just in case your figure has changed enough to require a different size pattern or different adjustments.

Try these tips for more precise measurements.

necessary to create patterns from scratch. Begin with the person in normal position and follow the series of steps outlined on pages 72–75. Enter the measurements in the chart on page 76.

The next step is to choose the correct size pattern. Since the chest or bust measurement is the most difficult to alter, try to select the pattern size that is closest to the subject's dimen-sions in this area. Bear in mind that it is usually easiest to narrow a pattern than to enlarge it, so if a choice has to be made select the pattern size that is slightly larger than body meas-urements, rather than a smaller size. Eliminate all pockets, pleats and decorative detail from the pattern.

The pattern pieces must then be individually measured and those measurements entered into the chart. When measuring the pattern, remember to go from stitching line to stitching line, not cutting line to cutting line. It is imperative to measure the pattern in accor-dance with the location at

(continued on page 77)

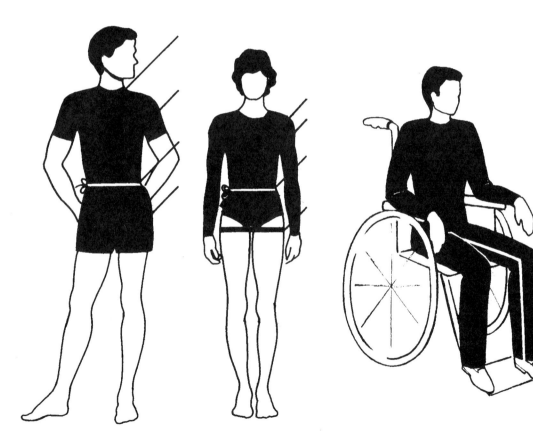

1. Height from top of head to floor (without shoes).

2. A. Back length (standing): Measure from bone at back of neck to waistline string.

2. B. Back length (for seated figure): Measure same as above.

3. Neck: Measure around the base of the neck (at Adam's apple for men).

4. High Bust (females only): measure directly under the arms above the breasts and around the back.

5. Chest/bust: Measure around the back and across the fullest part of the breast.

6. Waistline: determine the waistline measurement over the string (see Tips).

7. A. Hipline (seated): For the seated figure measure hipline horizontally around front and under buttocks.

   B. Hipline (standing): Measure hipline parallel to floor at fullest hip dimension (7-9 inches down from waist).

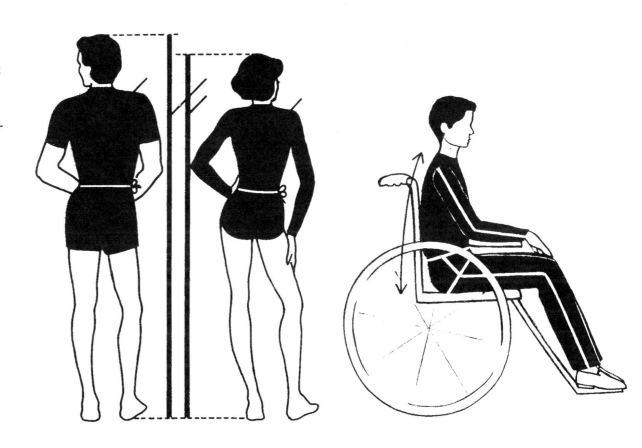

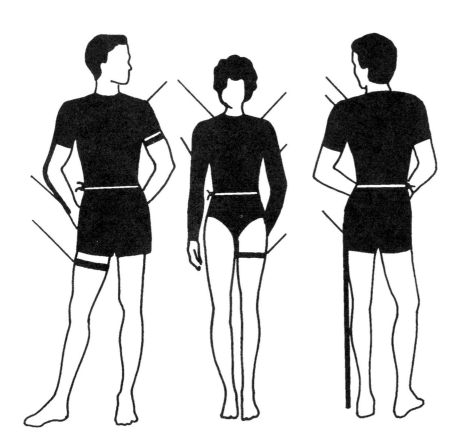

8. Front waist length: Measure from base of neck at shoulder to waist.

9. Shoulder to breast (female only): From shoulder to breast point.

10. Shoulder: Measure from neckline to shoulder bone.

11. Back Width: Measure across upper back at widest point (5-6 inches below base of neck).

12. Arm length: Measure from shoulder around bent elbow to wrist.

13. Shoulder to elbow (female only).

14. Upper Arm: Measure around widest part of upper arm.

15. Crotch Depth: From side waist to chair (use a hard ruler).

16. Front Crotch Length: Leaving string in position, measure front crotch length from a point of intersection of crotch seam to waistline string in front.

17. Back Crotch Length: Measure back crotch length from intersection of crotch seam to string in back.

18. Thigh: Measure horizontally around the widest part of the leg.

19. A. Outseam: Measure along the outer surface of the leg from waistline to ankle.

    B. Outseam (seated): Be sure to bend the tape measure as the body bends.

20. A. Inseam: Measure from crotch to ankle along the inner surface of the leg.

    B. Inseam (seated): Be sure to bend the tape measure as the body bends.

21. Uneven shoulders: Measure from shoulder in front to waistline over each breast.

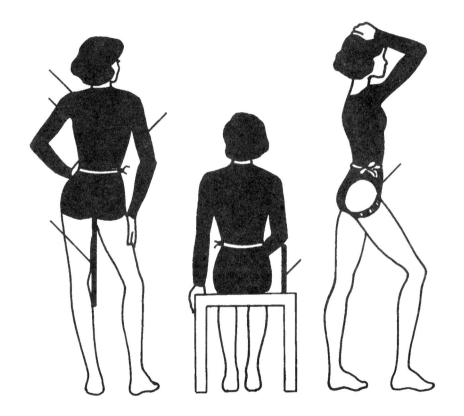

WHAT TO MEASURE	BODY	EASE	TOTAL	PATTERN	ADJUST-MENT
1. HEIGHT (without shoes)					
2. BACK WAIST LENGTH from prominent bone at back neck base to waist					
3. NECK around base of neck (around Adam's apple for men)		¾ "			
4. HIGH BUST (females only) directly under the arms, above the bust and around the back		1-1½ "			
5. BUST/CHEST around fullest part		2-4 "			
6. WAIST over the string		½-1"			
7. A. HIPLINE around fullest part while seated		3-5 "			
7. B. HIPLINE around fullest part while standing		2-4 "			
8. FRONT WAIST LENGTH from shoulder to neck base over bust point to waist		¼ "			
9. SHOULDER TO BREAST (females only) from shoulder at neck base to bust point		⅛"			
10. SHOULDER LENGTH from neck base to shoulder bone		0 "			
11. BACK WIDTH across the midback at widest point		¾-1"			

WHAT TO MEASURE	BODY	EASE	TOTAL	PATTERN	ADJUST-MENT
12. ARM LENGTH from shoulder bone to wristbone over slightly bent elbow		0 "			
13. SHOULDER TO ELBOW from end of shoulder to middle of slightly bent elbow		0 "			
14. UPPER ARM around arm at fullest part between shoulder and elbow		2-4 "			
15. CROTCH DEPTH height from seat to waist (seated)		1-1½ "			
16. FRONT CROTCH LENGTH from center front waist to intersection of crotch seams		1¼-1¾ "			
17. BACK CROTCH LENGTH from center back waist to intersection of crotch seams		1¾-2¼ "			
18. THIGH (standing) around the fullest part (seated)		2-4 " 3-5 "			
19. A. OUTSEAM (standing) along outside of leg from waistline to ankle		0 "			
19. B. OUTSEAM (seated) along outside of leg, bending tape measure as the body bends		0 "			
20. A. INSEAM (standing) from crotch to ankle along inner side of leg		0 "			
20. B. INSEAM (seated) crotch to ankle along inner side of leg, bending tape measure at knee		0 "			
21. A. FRONT WAIST, UNEVEN SHOULDERS from shoulder in front to waistline (left side)		¼ "			
21. B. FRONT WAIST, UNEVEN SHOULDERS from shoulder in front to waistline (right side)		¼ "			

which the same measurements were taken on the body. For example, if the subject's hip was measured at a point seven inches down from the string around the waistline, the pattern must also be measured seven inches down from the waistline.

As you enter the pattern measurements in Column 4, note the figures in the column marked EASE. *Ease is the amount of extra room at a given point in a garment that allows for wearing comfort.* If clothing had no ease, it would be skin-tight and look like a leotard. The ease figures have been filled in for you but they are subject to change based on the style of the garment. If, for instance, a pair of very full-cut harem-style pants was desired, four inches of ease in the hips would not be enough. Don't make the mistake of viewing these figures as absolute.

The next step is to find the total of columns 1 and 2, that is, body measurement plus ease and enter the totals into Column 3. Column 5 is the difference between Column 4 and Column 3

and represents the amount the pattern must be altered. Wherever there is a discrepancy of one-half inch or more, a pattern alteration should be made.

Before attempting pattern alterations, bear in mind that it is not difficult but it is exacting. Precision is the name of the game. Measurements should be exact, lines drawn ruler straight, and curves trued in with the appropriate tool. We suggest that if alterations are extensive or the pattern is a complex one, you should try a test garment of inexpensive fabric, such as unbleached muslin. This will let you see if the alterations were successful. If the pattern calls for a knit or stretch fabric, use a knit fabric with a similar amount of stretch for the test garment.

ALTERATIONS OF PANTS PATTERN FOR THE SEATED FIGURE

The most prominent changes in adapting the basic pants pattern for the seated figure take place

along the crotch line. The length of the center front and center back seams must be adjusted considerably to accommodate the seated posture. This alteration, however, should be done after the horizontal adjustments are made—that is, take in or let out the waist, hips, and thigh appropriately. Several books on the reading list will provide the how-tos for these simple pattern alterations. After you make the horizontal changes, vertical adjustments (crotch length, inseam/outseam length) can be made.

Using the chart, compare front crotch length of the subject to that of the pattern. Repeat, comparing back crotch length measurements. In virtually all cases, the pattern will be much too long in front and too short in back because of the altered body axis described in Chapter 3. Next, determine the exact amount of alteration from the last column on the chart.

Begin by removing all extensions for pockets and fly-front. The fly-front extension can be replaced after the pattern is corrected.

Most alterations are not difficult, but they must be made carefully.

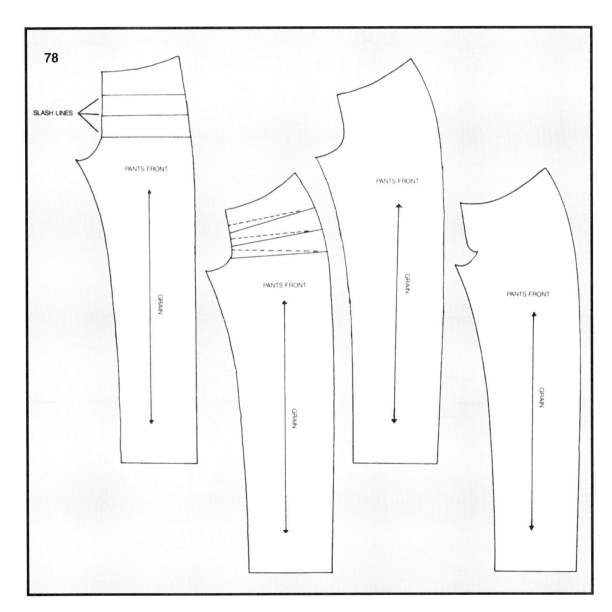

SLASH LINES

PANTS FRONT

GRAIN

PANTS FRONT

GRAIN

PANTS FRONT

GRAIN

PANTS FRONT

GRAIN

Pants Front

1. Slash the pattern along three parallel lines from center front to side seam *without cutting through side seam.* Divide the measurement of alteration in three.

2. Overlap the sections along center front by that amount until the desired crotch length is achieved. For example, if the amount of alteration is six inches, overlap each slash line by two inches.

3. True the pattern.

4. Draft new fly extension.

Pants Back

1. Slash pattern along three parallel lines from center back to side but *not through side seam*.

2. Spread pattern evenly until the center back is the desired length.

3. True in the seam lines.

4. Make final adjustments on inseam and outseam lengths at hemline if necessary.

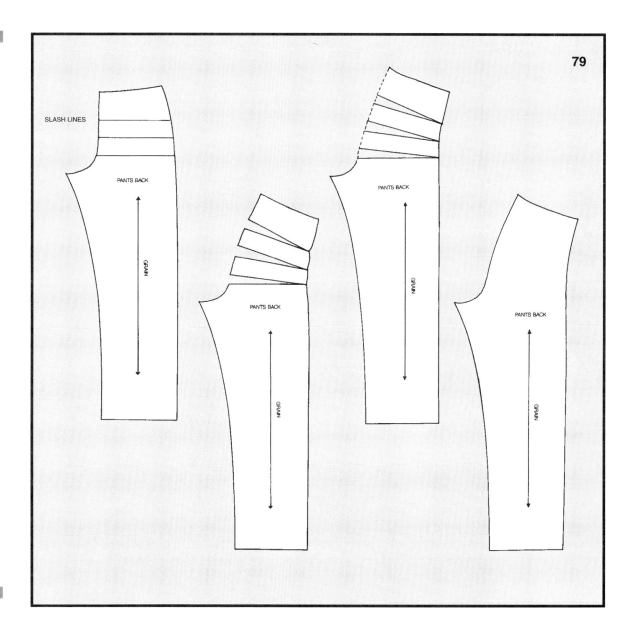

Alterations of the jacket pattern will give a better fit.

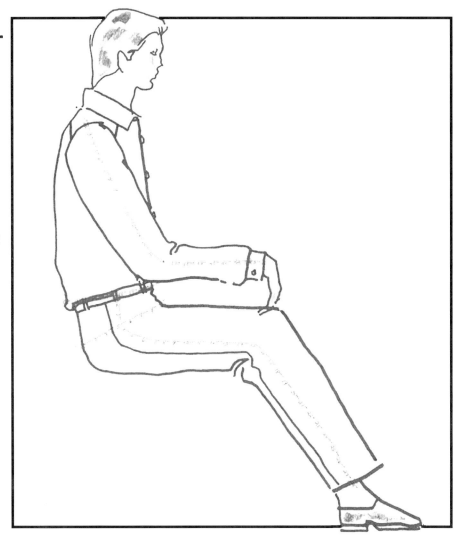

Figure 6-1. If a person spends most of his or her time in a wheelchair, measurements should be taken in that position.

ALTERING THE JACKET

Because the back of the seated person curves forward and is lengthened, the jacket strains across the shoulders, the armhole rides up and the neckline does not hug the neck of the wearer. To lengthen and widen the jacket back in the shoulder blade area, compare the body measurement plus ease with the pattern measurement and determine the amount of alteration. An additional measurement should be taken from the shoulder over the shoulder blade to the seat of the chair. This becomes the finished length of the jacket in back.

The following pattern alteration will result in a decreased neckline measurement. Therefore, the shape of the collar must change and the measurement of the collar must also decrease. This will result in a collar that hugs the neckline rather than standing away.

Jacket Back

1. Draw one line parallel to the center back from the middle of the shoulder seam to the hem. Draw a second line perpendicular to center back midway down the armhole. Slash along both lines.

2. Spread the pattern the appropriate amount (based on measurement chart) keeping points at hemline, shoulder, and center back in proper alignment. True the lines as illustrated.

3. Determine the length of the back from neck to the seat of the chair and add hem allowance.

4. Mark the width needed for hipline girth and true in line to the center back and along side seams.

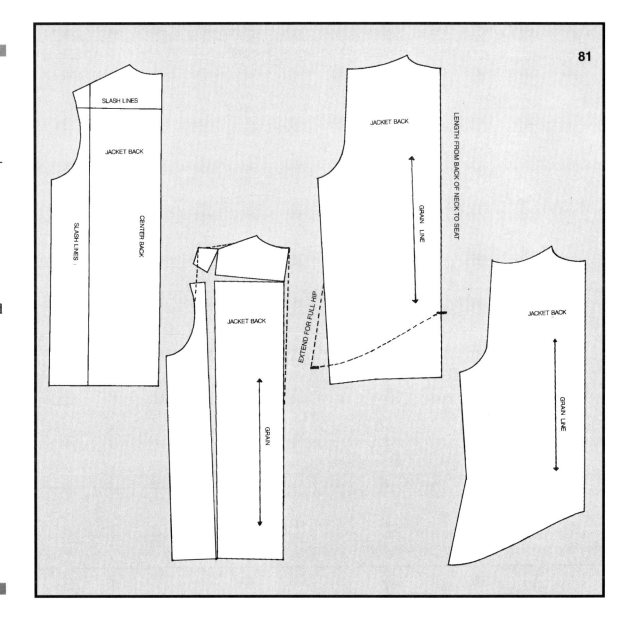

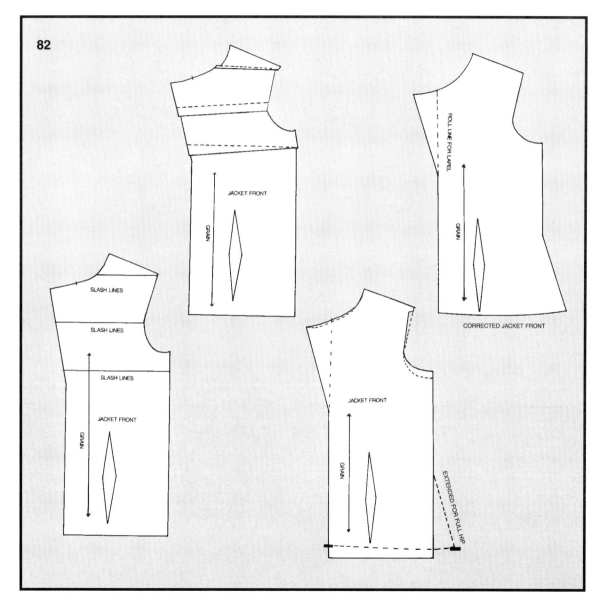

SLASH LINES

SLASH LINES

SLASH LINES

JACKET FRONT

GRAIN

JACKET FRONT

GRAIN

ROLL LINE FOR LAPEL

GRAIN

CORRECTED JACKET FRONT

JACKET FRONT

GRAIN

EXTENDED FOR FULL HIP

Jacket Front

1. To decrease the length in front of the jacket, slash the pattern in three places perpendicular to the grain line. Based on the measurements chart, determine the amount of change required in the length of the center front to waistline.

2. Overlap the slash lines as follows: *Top* approximately one half inch at neckline to one inch at armhole; *middle* evenly from armhole to lapel; *bottom* from nothing at side seam to approximately one inch at lapel. True in the lapel edge, the roll line and lower the armhole approximately one inch.

3. Determine the length to the hem of the jacket front and the width at the hip and blend the points. Make sure front and back match at the side seams.

Jacket Collar

1. Draw a slash line from the shoulder point at the outside of the collar to the center neckline edge of the collar.

2. Slash along line and overlap the neckline edge approximately one half inch.

3. True in the edges.

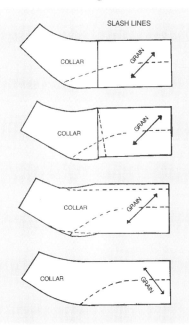

CORRECTED COLLAR PATTERN

Sleeves

Most of the time, the wheelchair-bound individual will have his or her elbows bent. The arms will rest either on the sides of the wheelchair or on the lap. Jacket sleeves then will look crumpled in the crook of the arm. To eliminate some of this fullness a simple alteration of the two-piece sleeve can be executed. After these alterations are complete, check to make sure the sleeve cap has not gotten larger or smaller.

1. Draw three slash lines perpendicular to the grain at the same points in both pattern pieces.

2. Slash along the lines from the front of the sleeve to the back but not through the back. Overlap approximately one-half inch at each point. Be sure both parts are exactly the same.

3. True in the curves.

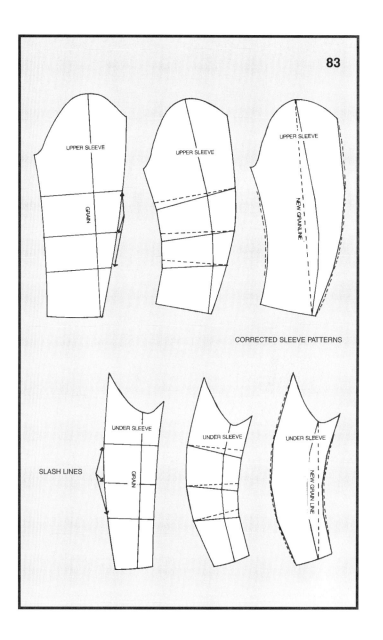

CORRECTED SLEEVE PATTERNS

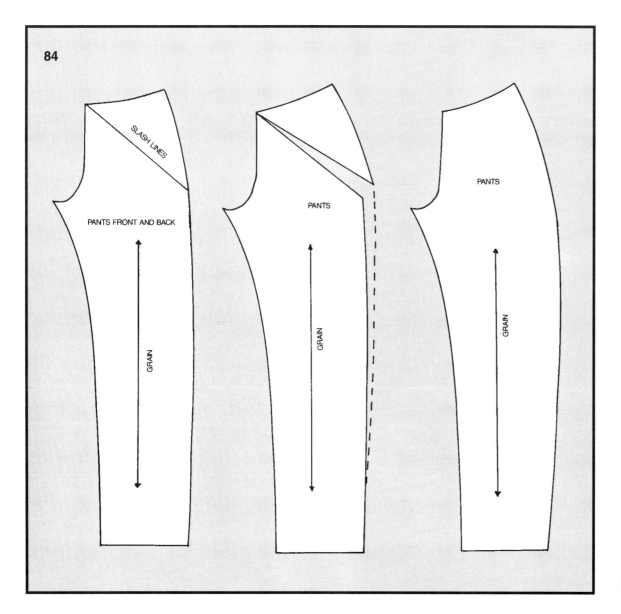

84

SLASH LINES

PANTS FRONT AND BACK

GRAIN

PANTS

GRAIN

PANTS

GRAIN

PATTERN ALTERATIONS FOR SCOLIOSIS

Pants or Skirt

To correct a pattern to accommodate one high and one low hip, the following procedure should be taken.

First, measure the distance from the waistline to the low hip along the side seam and repeat for the high hip.

Whether working with pants or a skirt, the procedure is the same. Remember to treat the pattern back in the same way as the front.

1. Draw a diagonal line from the higher hip to the opposite side of the waist and slash.

2. Raise the appropriate amount and true in the line.

3. Do the same for the back sections on the corresponding side.

4. True in all darts along a horizontal plane (one dart will, of course, be longer than the other).

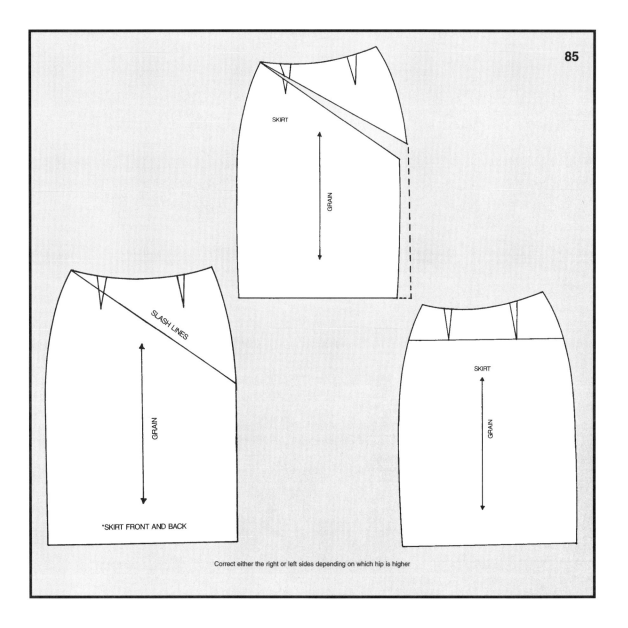

Correct either the right or left sides depending on which hip is higher

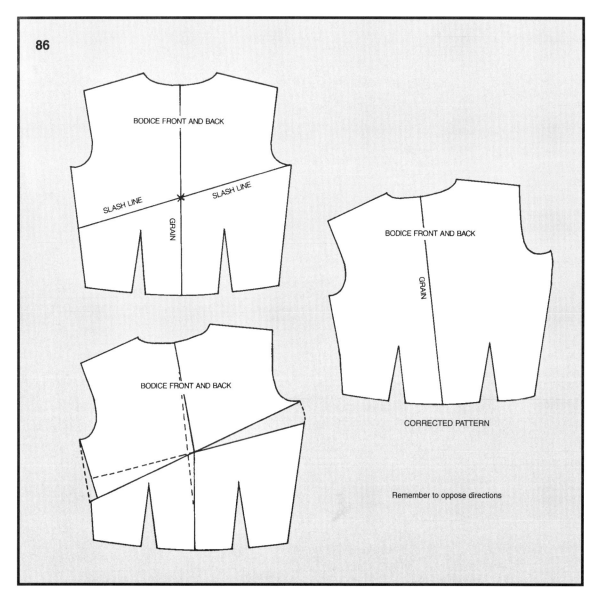

BODICE FRONT AND BACK

SLASH LINE   SLASH LINE

GRAIN

BODICE FRONT AND BACK

GRAIN

BODICE FRONT AND BACK

CORRECTED PATTERN

Remember to oppose directions

Bodice

Procedure for the bodice adaptation is similar to the skirt or pants. Using the measurement chart, determine the difference in length between the higher shoulder to waist and the lower shoulder to waist.

1. Draw a line from the underarm point on the higher shoulder side to approximately midway along the side seam in the opposite side; slash along this line.

2. Overlap the pattern appropriately in the lower side and spread on the higher side.

3. True in the lines.

PATTERN ALTERATION FOR KYPHOSIS

Kyphosis (humpback) is not as prevalent as it was when tuberculosis existed in epidemic proportions. Nevertheless, many individuals experience spinal curvature and require pattern adjustments for proper fit

Bodice Front

To alter a basic bodice for kyphosis, first determine the measurement from neck to waist in front and back.

1. Slash bodice through the center of the bustline dart perpendicular to grain.
2. Overlap center front the appropriate amount and draw a line from neck to waist. This becomes the new center front.
3. Underarm will be stitched on original lines. Realign the waist dart if necessary, so that it parallels new center front line.

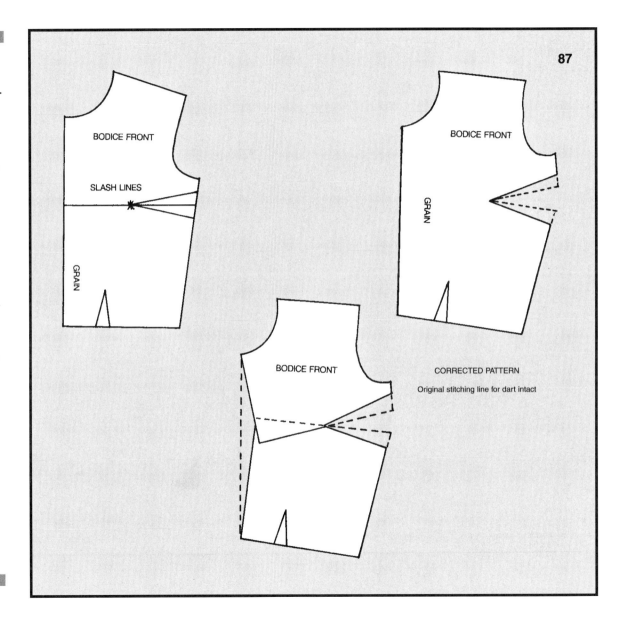

BODICE FRONT

SLASH LINES

GRAIN

BODICE FRONT

GRAIN

BODICE FRONT

CORRECTED PATTERN

Original stitching line for dart intact

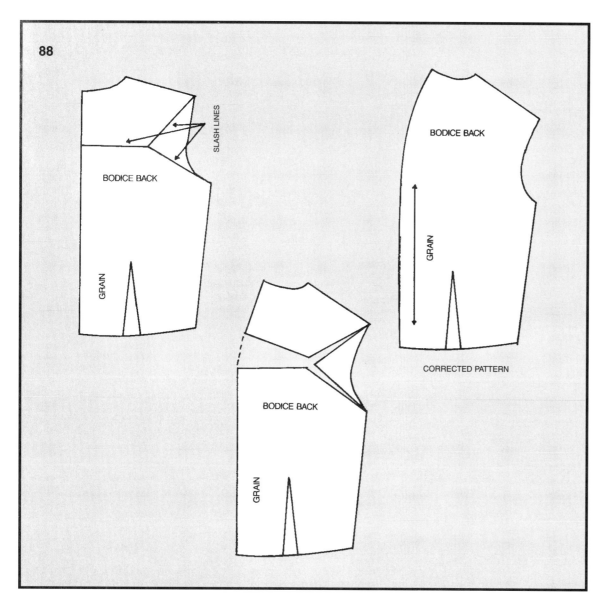

SLASH LINES

BODICE BACK

GRAIN

BODICE BACK

GRAIN

BODICE BACK

GRAIN

BODICE BACK

GRAIN

CORRECTED PATTERN

Bodice Back

1. Mark slash lines perpendicular to the grain and up to the shoulder, then out to the armhole at the side seam but not through the shoulder or side.

2. Raise the back the appropriate amount, allowing the pattern to spread as evenly as possible in the other two areas.

3. True in the line along the center back.

ADJUSTMENTS TO READY-TO-WEAR GARMENTS

Action Pleats, Flanges

Action pleats are a type of release pleat that can be sewn into the back armhole of a jacket, blouse, or coat. They add great comfort to the clothing worn by crutch users and the wheelchair-bound who propel themselves manually. To make an action pleat:

1. Open the armhole seam in jacket back up to the shoulder and down to the side.

2. Open the shoulder seam and side seam three inches each.

3. To make a pattern for the insert, place a folded piece of fabric against shoulder seam and trace the shape of the armhole, shoulder and side seam. Add seam allowances and cut.

4. Stitch one curved edge of insert to the sleeve, the other to the armhole of the jacket.

5. Stitch insert across the bottom.

6. Restitch shoulder and side seams through all thicknesses.

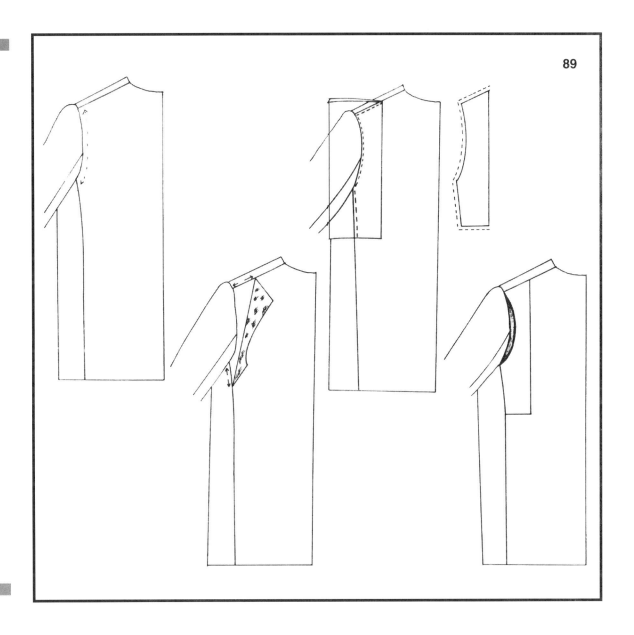

Gussets

Stitching a gusset into an underarm or crotch area to provide more freedom of movement is a simple operation. A diamond-shaped piece of fabric is inserted into the underarm or crotch seam after each seam has been opened.

1. Open seams 4½ " in all directions.

2. Draw a diamond-shaped insert 4 " on each side and 7 " along the center. Add seam allowances and cut out insert.

3. Stitch insert into garment.

Gussets can provide additional freedom of movement in ready-to-wear garments.

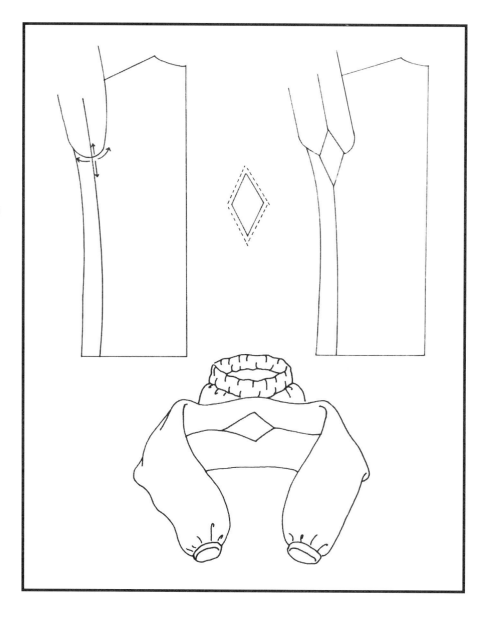

SELECTION OF FABRIC

When an artist decides upon a medium for a particular work, in some ways he or she decides how viewers are to perceive that work. The oft-used phrase "The medium is the message" is as appropriate for the painter or sculptor as it is for the clothing designer. In the case of the latter, the material, whether cloth, leather, or fur, is the medium.

Many factors including appearance, comfort, and performance, must be taken into consideration in the selection of appropriate material for a particular design. For many people, comfort and performance are less important than the beauty of the fabric. For example, a woman to whom fashion is more important than function will have no problem in choosing a stiff silk taffeta dress that wrinkles when she sits.

The fashionable quality of the garment is indeed primary, for both the able-bodied and the disabled, but it is imperative that the person who sits in a wheelchair all day be comfortable. The fabric that undergoes constant stress as this person propels the wheelchair must be strong enough to endure the strain. Therefore, the factors of aesthetics, comfort, and performance will be addressed separately, but they must all work together.

As has been mentioned previously, an understanding and assessment of the subject's physical appearance, limitations, and requirements should always be foremost when making a design or construction decision. This assessment will be helpful in determining the aesthetics of the fabric as well as its functional aspects. Let subject's skin and hair tones dictate the color of the fabric. Body structure, including weight, may influence the choice of pattern on the cloth. Guidelines for color and pattern selections were discussed in Chapter 2 and can also be found in many commercially available books that offer advice on color choices, based not only on physical characteristics but, believe it or not, on personality as well. The functional aspects of the fabric can be divided into two main categories—comfort and performance. Although both categories are important to the disabled person, some of the properties inherent in each may be deemed mandatory.

Performance

By the term performance we mean all issues involving the upkeep and wearability of the cloth. Some of the factors that affect performance include:

Durability

This is an area where comfort and aesthetics may conflict with function. Natural fibers are considered preferable to man-made in terms of beauty and comfort; however, synthetics have much greater yarn strength and better resistance to abrasion. The solution is to select a fabric that combines the best qualities of both natural and man-made fibers. In other words, a 50-50 or 60-40 blend of cotton and polyester will

Keep the wearer's preferences in mind when choosing fabrics.

Easy-care fabrics are a practical choice.

have the properties of a synthetic that enable it to resist abrasion and withstand wear but it will also have some of the properties of 100% cotton, allowing for the fabric to "breathe" and to be soft and comfortable to wear.

Another consideration is tightness of the weave. The rule of thumb is the tighter the tougher. For the person who wears leg braces, the fabric requirement for trousers should be a blend of polyester or nylon with washed wool or cotton in a very tight weave. This fabric will resist the abrasion caused by the braces much more readily than a loose weave or knit. In using crutches, propelling a wheelchair, reaching, or struggling to put clothing on, the strain on fabric is tremendous and durability is a "must." Again, the need must be analyzed. The person with a brace needs a tightly woven fabric. The immobile person who has trouble putting on his clothes needs a stretch knit. The stretch in the fabric will allow the garment to "give" as much as one and a half times its width.

This is certainly helpful when limited dexterity makes putting on clothing difficult. Stretch wovens have become available and these are particularly useful for pants for the seated person. The stretch factor provides extra comfort, yet the fabric appears trim and business-like.

Concern should be given to the potential shrinkage of a particular fiber. Here again, a blend of natural fibers (wool, cotton) with polyester or nylon will lend itself best to repeated launderings. Pure cotton or wool will shrink more than a blend. There are many shrinkage control finishes that can be applied to natural fibers to stabilize the fabric.

Maintenance

This is an extremely important consideration in fabricating clothing for the disabled. Because a disabled person normally has few well-fitting clothes, those garments are laundered much more often than the average person's. In addition, problems of incontinence

may also increase the number of launderings.

Obviously, garments worn and washed frequently need to be easily cared for—that is, machine washable, dryable and wrinkle-resistant. Suggested fabrics include cotton/polyester blends, washable woolens, and no-iron cottons. Soil-release finishes are also a help with stains and general laundering.

Odor Retention

If odors due to excessive perspiration or lack of bladder control are a problem, garment fabrics should be selected with this in mind. Note that natural fibers generally do not retain body odors the way man-made fibers, especially polyesters, do. Antibacterial finishes are available and retard growth of odor-causing bacteria.

Safety/Flammability

Immobility presents a certain set of safety concerns, one of them the inability to react quickly to fire. It is a good precaution to use flame retardant fabrics or fabrics treated with flame resistant finishes when clothing people in this category. Many such fabrics must, however, be laundered according to specific manufacturer's instructions if they are to keep their safety features. Fabrics can be treated with spray now available to help make them flame retardant.

Comfort

Comfort is the ease in wear of a garment and is determined both by style and fit of the article of clothing as well as the properties inherent in the fabric itself. On a psychological level, comfort can be assessed by the degree of positive feeling the wearer gets from this clothing. Some of the physical concerns related to comfort will be addressed.

Thermal Insulation

Warmth does not necessarily come from weight. That is, it is not necessary to wear a heavy coat in order to be warm. Fabric with a brushed finish or surface nap or with fluffy textures have the ability to trap air which adds to warmth. Use fleece or fluffy blanket-like fabrics for warmth without weight. Quilted fabrics filled with down or poly-fill are another choice for outer garments. Layering wool alternating with cotton also helps keep heat in and cold out.

Texture

This is an important issue in terms of comfort. People with thin, sensitive skin require soft, fleecy fabrics as opposed to the harshness of a crisp worsted. The less surface contact a fabric has with the skin, the more comfortable it is. Fabric with raised surfaces, such as terry cloth velours, brushed cotton, or fleece are much easier to wear.

Absorbency

The ability to soak up moisture greatly affects comfort. When a fabric can absorb perspiration and admit air the skin can breathe more easily and body heat can be regulated. Natural fibers have much greater absorbency proper-

ties than do synthetics; synthetics make the body colder when outside temperatures are low, and warmer when they are high. Fabrics with lower absorbency also have the tendency to become filled with static electricity and then cling to the body. Cotton knits and sweatshirt fleeces are good choices when absorbency is desirable.

A Closing Note

With all of these concerns in mind, the design process has already begun—a process that is no different for designing clothes for the disabled than for designing a car! Hopefully, this book has provided some guidance in evaluating individual problems and some hints about materials and basic design principles. But more than offering a series of "how-tos" we hope that we have offered the disabled community and the public at large the realization that fashion is available to everyone—that no matter what the physical limitation, we all have the capacity to look great!

READING LIST

BOOKS

Armstrong, Helen Joseph. *Draping for Apparel Design.* New York: Fairchild Publications, Inc., 2000.

_____. *Patternmaking for Fashion Design.* 3rd ed. Upple Saddle River, NJ: Prentice Hall, 2000.

Bevlin, Marjorie Elliott. *Design through Discovery: An Introduction.* 6th ed. Orlando, FL: Harcoart, Brace & Co., 1984. Out of Print.

Chambers, Helen G. and Verna Moulton. *Clothing Selection Fashions, Fabric.* Philadelphia: Lippincott, 1979. Out of Print.

Chowdhary, U. *Clothing for Special Needs: An Annotated Bibliography.* Mount Pleasant, MI: Central Michigan University Printing Services, 2002.

_____. *Functional Clothing, Body Comfort, and Special Needs.* Mount Pleasant, MI: Central Michigan University Printing Services, 2002.

Davis, Marian L. *Visual Design in Dress.* 3rd ed. Upper Saddle River, NJ: Prentice Hall, 1996.

Disabled Living Foundation. *All Dressed Up.* London: Disabled Living Foundation, n.d.

_____. *Wheelchair Information.* London: Disabled Living Foundation, n.d.

Eicher, Joanne B., Sandra Lee Evenson, and Hazel A. Lutz. *The Visible Self: Global Perspectives on Dress, Culture, and Society.* 2nd ed. New York: Fairchild Publications, Inc., 2000.

Fraser, Kennedy. *The Fashionable Mind.* Boston: David R. Godine, Inc., 1984. Out of Print.

Hale, Glorya, ed. *The Source Book for the Disabled: An Illustrated Guide.* New York: Paddington Press, 1979. Out of Print.

Hoffman, Adeline M. *Clothing for the Handicapped,the Aged, and Other People with Special Needs.* Springfield, IL: Charles C. Thomas Publisher, 1979. Out of Print.

Horn, Marilyn J. *The Second Skin: An Interdisciplinary Study of Clothing.* 3rd ed. Boston: Houghton Mifflin Company, 1981. Out of Print.

Kennedy, Evelyn S. *Clothing Accessibility: A Lesson Plan to Aid the Disabled and the Elderly.* Groton, CT: P.R.I.D.E., 1987.

_____. *Dressing With Pride, Vol. 1 Clothing Changes for Special Needs.* Groton, CT: P.R.I.D.E., 1981.

Kernaleguen, Anne. *Clothing Designs for the Handicapped.* Alberta: The University of Alberta Press, 1980. Out of Print.

Lurie, Alison. *The Language of Clothes.* New York: Henry Holt & Company, 2000.

MacDonald, Nora A. *Principles of Flat Pattern Design.* 3rd ed. New York: Fairchild Publications, Inc., 2002.

May, Elizabeth Eckhart, Neva R. Waggoner, and Eleanor Boettke Hotte. *Independent Living for the Handicapped and the Elderly.* Boston: Houghton Mifflin Company, 1974. Out of Print.

Sargent, Jean Vieth. *An Easier Way: Handbook for the Elderly and Handicapped.* Ames, IA: Iowa State University Press, 1981. Out of Print.

Saunders, Janice S. *Sewing for Dummies.* New York: John Wiley & Sons, Inc., 1999.

Soto, Anne Marie. *Simplicity's Simply the Best Sewing Book.* New York: Simplicity Pattern Co., Inc., 1999.

BOOKLETS

Brown, Pamela J., Laura Sternweis, and Janis Stone. *Consumer Choices: Selecting Clothes for Older People in Your Care.* Cooperative Extension Service, Iowa State University, Ames, IA 50010, Extension Bulletin:
Consumer Choices: Clothing Ideas for People with Special Needs, 1993

Disabled Living Foundation, 380-384 Harrow Road, London W9 2HU, England. (When ordering send a bank draft in British currency—pounds).
Design Advice, 2.50 pounds
Equipment that Needs Designing, 1.00 pounds
Choosing a Bra, 2.50 pounds

Clothing and Footwear for Sensitive Skin, 2.50 pounds
Clothing Ideas for People Who Rip Clothing, 2.50 pounds
Clothing Ideas for Wheelchair Users, 2.50 pounds
Clothing Services, 1.00 pounds
Dressing for Warmth, 2.50 pounds
Equipment to Assist with Dressing and Putting on Footwear, 2.50 pounds
Footwear Adaptations for Difficult Feet, 2.50 pounds
Footwear for Odd-sized Feet, 2.50 pounds
Footwear for People with Minor Feet Problems or Medical Conditions, 2.50 pounds
Footwear for Swollen Feet, 2.50 pounds
Slippers, 2.50 pounds

Hall, Vondalyn. *Appearance Makes a Difference in Later Years.* Auburn University Cooperative Extension Service, Circular HE-143, 1978, 4 pp. Printed in large type for easy reading by older adults.

Hom, Mol and Janis Stone. *Clothing Ideas for People with Back Irregularities.* Cooperative Extension Service, Iowa State University, Ames, IA 50010, 2000.

Stone, Janis. *Clothing Ideas for the Mobility Impaired.* Cooperative Extension Service, Iowa State University, Ames, IA 50010, Extension Bulletins:
Clothing Ideas for People with Arthritis, 2000
Special Clothing Needs: A Few Causes of Disabling Conditions, 2001
Special Needs Clothing Sources, 2001

INDEX

CL

646.
401
CHA